D0041658

Measure of the Heart

Measure of the Heart

A Father's Alzheimer's,
A Daughter's Return

Mary Ellen Geist

Foreword by Oliver Sacks

SPRINGBOARD PRESS

NEW YORK BOSTON

Springboard Press
Hachette Book Group USA
237 Park Avenue, New York, NY 10017

Visit our Web site at www.HachetteBookGroupUSA.com

Springboard Press is an imprint of Grand Central Publishing.
The Springboard name and logo are trademarks of Hachette Book Group USA, Inc.

Printed in the United States of America

First Edition: August 2008

10 9 8 7 6 5 4 3 2 1

Library of Congress Cataloging-in-Publication Data

Geist, Mary Ellen.
    Measure of the heart : a father's Alzheimer's, a daughter's return / Mary Ellen
Geist. — 1st ed.
        p. cm.
    Includes bibliographical references.
    ISBN-13: 978-0-446-58092-2
    ISBN-10: 0-446-58092-9
    1. Geist, Mary Ellen. 2. Geist, Woody—Mental health. 3. Alzheimer's disease—
Patients—United States—Biography. 4. Radio journalists—United States—
Biography. 5. Alzheimer's disease—Patients—Care. 6. Adult children of aging
parents—United States—Biography. I. Title.

RC523.2.G45 2008
362.196'8310092—dc22
    [B]   2007047221

Book design by Giorgetta Bell McRee

For my father, Woody, for my mother, Rosemary,
and for everyone who loves someone who has Alzheimer's.

Contents

Foreword

by Oliver Sacks

A LONG LIFETIME OF EXPERIENCE CAN BRING wisdom and calm, so that the aged are often revered and play crucial roles as elders in many communities. But aging can also bring about tragic impairments of memory and mental power. Prior to the twentieth century, "senility," it seems, was relatively rare—or perhaps it was simply less recognized as such, since "senile" parents and grandparents continued to live as an integral part of the family and the community; they were not singled out, pathologized, and put away as they are so often now.

I was reminded of this, very movingly, a few years ago when I visited Guam, a place where there is an endemic neurological disease that sometimes causes an Alzheimer's-like dementia. But the people afflicted with this in Guam are, by and large, not institutionalized as they would probably be in the United States. They remain part of their families and their communities until the end. Our own culture, generally, has little patience, little tolerance, little feeling for those who are old or sick—and now, as the average lifespan has moved toward eighty, more and more of us are living long enough to develop Alzheimer's or other types of dementia.

There is now, as we are acutely aware, a veritable epidemic of Alzheimer's (not a new condition, only a new name for what used to be called "senility"). In the United States alone, it has been reckoned, there are more than five million people with Alzheimer's, and all of them, sooner or later, will need special, painstaking care. At the moment, medications have only a transient effect, and none of them can prevent or slow the advance of the disease. While economists and healthcare administrators must think of the huge economic and societal burdens this inevitably imposes, the rest of us must think in individual, human terms. How, in our culture, will people with Alzheimer's be cared for and at what human cost to the caregivers?

Mary Ellen Geist was an award-winning reporter and anchor at several radio stations in Los Angeles, San Francisco, and New York. She was in her forties, working at WCBS in Manhattan, at the top of a brilliant career, when she decided to give all that up and return to her childhood home to help with the care of her father, Woody, who had developed Alzheimer's several years earlier. Not that Woody was "difficult"—he was almost invariably sweet, affectionate, thoughtful—but he had lost almost all memory of his previous life, could not remember from second to second where he was or what he had been doing, could not dress by himself, and was almost totally dependent on others' help. The burden of this caregiving fell on his wife, Rosemary, and she was no longer able to handle the overwhelming task by herself.

"In the winter of 2005," Mary Ellen writes, "I moved my luggage, a few books, and my computer up to my room. . . . there was no place for the things I owned in my former life. . . . I had removed myself from the adrenaline rush and the sometimes cold and ruthless world of reporting and anchoring the news. I was now living my life by totally new rules. Instead of living in the world of broadcast journalism, I was being given a chance to live in a place of total love and caring for someone else."

So Mary Ellen Geist starts her tender, but tough-minded, and beautifully written memoir, *Measure of the Heart*.

But total love and caring for someone else, especially if the someone is already quite demented and is gradually, inexorably, going downhill, was to be anything but easy. Her mother had been, in effect, on duty, on call, twenty-four hours a day, and even when Mary Ellen divided the tasks of caregiving with her mother, there was little freedom for either of them. Someone had to be with Woody all the time—preventing him from wandering off and getting lost, making sure he took his medicine, reminding him to finish dressing.

Caregiving of this sort, which can involve backbreaking physical exertion as well as a constant, almost telepathic sensitivity to what is going on in a mind now less and less able to communicate its thoughts, less and less able to have clear thoughts, can make the caregiver ill with stress, grind one to the ground. As a physician, I see this all too often, especially when a spouse has been disabled by a stroke or neurological disease: sometimes the stress is so great that an elderly husband or wife will sacrifice their own health and die before the loved one they are caring for. This is why outside help, if only for a few hours a week, may also be crucial.

What made fulltime caring at home for Woody possible were a number of factors, including financial resources and the extraordinarily generous, giving, and loving character not only of Mary Ellen and her mother, but of Woody himself, who retained his emotional depth and easygoing nature despite his ever-advancing dementia. Woody was able, in this way, to return their love in full, and without this their task would have been much harder, less joyful, for them. (Sadly, this is not always the case; there may be distressing personality changes and even violent behavior in some people with Alzheimer's, especially as the disease progresses.)

Sometimes people with dementia may get terrifyingly confused and disoriented. When Woody felt lost and uncertain, he could call Mary Ellen—not by name, as he had forgotten which of his three daughters she was, and so he would call, "Daughter, where are you?" But it was not just the familiar, trusted, loved presence of his wife and daughter that grounded Woody. There was another very special factor in his case, and it was this which Mary Ellen emphasized when she first wrote to me:

> The plaque has apparently invaded a large amount of his brain, and he can't remember much of anything about his life. However, he remembers the baritone part to almost every song he has ever sung. He has performed with a twelve-man a cappella singing group for almost forty years. . . . Music is one of the only things that keeps him grounded in this world.
>
> He has no idea what he did for a living, where he is living now, or what he did ten minutes ago. Almost every memory is gone. Except for the music. In fact, he opened for the Radio City Music Hall Rockettes in Detroit this past November. . . . The evening he performed, he had no idea how to tie a tie . . . he got lost on the way to the stage—but the performance? Perfect. . . . He performed beautifully and remembered all the parts and words.

There was not just the a cappella group; the Geists were a singing family. Singing together, improvising, harmonizing, were central in the Geist household while Mary Ellen and her sisters were growing up, and it is still central to the family. Mary Ellen, Woody, and Rosemary came to visit me in New York on one occasion, and Woody was whistling "Somewhere Over the Rainbow" as he came in, so I asked him to sing it. Rosemary and Mary Ellen joined in, and the three of them sang beautifully, each harmonizing in different ways. When Woody sang, he showed all the expressions, emotions, and postures appropriate to the song, and to performing in a group—turning to the others, awaiting their cues, and so on. His musicality, like his civility and equanimity, was completely intact, and when he sang, he seemed to be completely present, to come together and bypass his dementia (though as soon as the singing ended, the dementia was evident again). I was impressed by this and wrote about it in a chapter on music and dementia in my book *Musicophilia*. But there was much more to Woody's story, and now his daughter has written eloquently of a whole family living with dementia.

Measure of the Heart is a double story, as its subtitle (*A Father's Alzheimer's, A Daughter's Return*) indicates. Mary Ellen Geist provides, first, a richly detailed, sympathetic portrait of her father's battle with a cruel dementia, a battle which, though tragic and painful, is at times high-spirited and even humorous. But this is equally the story of a daughter searching to find the right words, the right actions, the right feelings, for a father who is declining, to establish a relationship with a father who cannot recall her name, and to give dignity and reassurance to a man who gets lost in his own house.

There is no formula here—there is only tact, delicacy, sympathy, intuition. Coming from a competitive, ambitious, noisy, and often heartless world, Mary Ellen had to learn, as her mother had already learned, what she calls "the measure of the heart." Mary Ellen's return home to help a lost father became a transforming experience for her as well, a journey into her own almost forgotten deeper self. Alzheimer's disease can be a great destroyer, not only of those who have it, but of their families as well. But sometimes, by a poignant paradox, Alzheimer's may bring a family together and bring about the deepest relationship any of them have known.

—Dr. Oliver Sacks

Life's a voyage that's homeward bound.

—HERMAN MELVILLE

Prologue

One More Year

It was December 12, 2004. I flew home from New York to be in Michigan for the weekend to celebrate my father's birthday. He was turning seventy-eight. My mother bought a small cake for him and put a tiny candle in it. My sisters, my mother, and various friends gave him lots of cards.

He peeled the envelopes open slowly, sometimes upside down, and opened the cards from the back to the front. Then he handed the cards to my mother or to me to read to him. He leaned in to the table with his head cocked at an angle—a new stance he had acquired lately—and watched the proceedings around him with a quizzical look on his face.

He looked at the birthday cake and the glowing candle and then looked back at us. Several minutes seemed to pass as the flame burned down and wax began to drip onto the frosting. Then we realized: he didn't know what to do. So we told him, "You're supposed to blow out the candle and make a wish." He didn't seem to understand the concept. We demonstrated blowing. Finally, we saw a glimmer of recognition in his eyes. He seemed to understand the concept of blowing out a candle, but we realized he didn't understand the idea of "wish." We explained that it's something you want now or in the future. A knowing look appeared on his face, and he blew out the candle in one swift breath. The *whh* noise resounded triumphantly in the room. A thin trail of white smoke snaked up from the center of the cake, then disappeared into the air. We asked him what he had wished for. He said, "One more year."

We first suspected that my father, Woody Geist, had Alzheimer's in the winter of 1994. He is one of the estimated 5.1 million people in the United States who currently suffer from this disease. The Alzheimer's Association says that figure could reach 16 million people over the age of sixty-five by the year 2050.

When my father learned that his brain had begun to fill with plaque, he wrote letters to each of us—his three daughters—explaining what he knew about his disease and telling us how much he loved us. He said he knew the coming years would be more difficult for our mother than they would be for him. He told us what a wonderful life he felt he had lived and how happy we had made him. He said he and Mom were going to enjoy life as much as possible until his disease prevented them from doing so. He informed his close friends of his diagnosis, including the group of men with whom he sings a cappella music on a weekly basis. He said he planned to keep up with as many of his regular activities as long as he could. He told everyone he saw on a routine basis, including members of his church, that he hoped this approach to his disease would not burden them.

At first, it was slow—memory lapses and difficulty remembering people's names. Then he started getting lost while he was driving. My mother took him to an expert, who performed a barrage of tests. The problem, as I understand it, is that you can't definitively identify the disease until the person is dead and the brain can be thoroughly examined. But the doctors informed us that they were 99 percent sure: Alzheimer's.

Now what? My parents decided to be aggressive in treating the disease with the latest drugs and began enrolling my father in clinical trials. He began taking the drug called Aricept as soon as it was available.

My father began an epic battle with his own brain. It is a battle that has continued for more than a decade, and only recently has he begun to lose this battle.

Daughter, Where Are You?

I AM ONE OF MILLIONS OF PEOPLE who uproot their lives to help take care of parents who need them. Alzheimer's disease is drawing more and more people home. No statistics are available right now on how many people quit their jobs to help take care of their parents, but it's presumed that more women than men are choosing to do this each year. The National Alliance for Caregiving and AARP, in a 2004 study, reported that women accounted for 71 percent of those devoting forty or more hours per week to the task of caregiving. As Jane Gross reported in the *New York Times* in November 2005, among those with the greatest burden of care, regardless of sex, 88 percent either take leaves of absence, quit, or retire from their jobs.

It is safe to say that each day in the United States dozens of daughters and sons are contemplating transferring jobs or quitting them altogether to respond to the needs of aging parents. Some are moving themselves or their entire families from the East to the West Coast or vice versa; others are moving from urban centers to small towns in Iowa, Ohio, or Michigan to help with the daily care of a mother or a father. As I write this, cars and planes and trains are taking adult children back to their family homes as they take a leap like I did: to help take on the task of caregiving.

If you look closely, you will see them at doctor's offices,

accompanying parents to appointments. You will see them dropping off their parents at day care centers. You will see them trying to maneuver their Alzheimer's-afflicted mother or father through the aisles at neighborhood grocery stores.

We find each other easily in crowds. The daughters—we look each other in the eye, as if to ask, Where's your husband? Where are your children? Are you single, too? Did you leave your life in a big city to come home to help your parents, too?

We often have unkempt hair, no makeup, and a look of exasperation in our eyes. We are trying to hide the fact that we have just wrestled our parents into tennis shoes after coaxing them to finish their cereal and explaining to them what pills are and why they have to take them, and where we are going today. I see faces that look like my mother's that seem to say, This shouldn't be happening to me. I don't deserve this. This was supposed to be the best time in our lives. . . .

The daughters whose eyes I meet—we hold our parents' arms cautiously, always on the lookout for uneven sidewalks or pavement. We have developed a new awareness of The Curb, knowing that our parents' limbs might not do what they want them to do. Sometimes, we look very, very lost. Almost as lost as our parents who have Alzheimer's.

Most of the time, we meet each other's glances and then look away. We get into our cars and drive away. Some of us are going off to part-time jobs or back to our homes to be with our children or husbands. Or we are heading off to a coffee shop to have a few moments alone to breathe before we go back to the task of caregiving. Some of us will head back to the family home to do daily chores and comfort the wives or husbands of our parents with Alzheimer's, who are suffering from broken hearts and whose lives are slowly being chipped away by the disease.

Some of us realize that we are coming home not only to help do the remembering for our Alzheimer's-afflicted parents, but also to remember something very important about ourselves. We are coming home to learn how to measure our lives by new standards that we've never explored before, to measure our lives in a different way. Instead of defining ourselves by our careers, we're defining ourselves by the amount of love our hearts can hold.

When I first came home to Michigan, my father told me every day how much he loved me. That in itself made coming home worthwhile. But I also realized that he was beginning to be unclear about where to place me. One day, as we drove in the car along country roads near our home, he turned to me and said, "Are you the youngest one?" When something like this happens with a person living with Alzheimer's, at first, you feel this pang of pain that your own father can't remember when you were born or where you belong in the family. Then you tell yourself not to be hurt, because it's not that your father has forgotten you. It's that Alzheimer's has stolen his memories away. You say it over and over: It's not my father. It's his disease. Then you tell yourself once again to get over it, because each moment is so fleeting, and you must make the most of what you have now.

Right after I got home, I trained myself to respond appropriately to questions like this. Now I answer, "No, Dad, I'm the middle one," without feeling like crying, and I take the opportunity to tell him about our family, about when my older sister, Alison, was born, and when I was born, and when my younger sister, Libby, was born. I describe our birth order the same way I would explain a news item to him or how to work a can opener. He's always so glad to hear about the history of our family, and each time it is brand new. After I tell him that each of us went to college and what has transpired since then in our lives, he says, "Aren't we lucky?"

Lately he has been dropping articles and prepositions and the use of proper names. So now, when he is looking for me in the house, he says, "Daughter, where are you?" It's another one of his magnificent coping mechanisms. It's a way to say, I know you. I may not be able to be specific about your name because of my disease, but I know you.

Now, when my father calls out in the house, "Daughter, where are you?" I answer, "I'm right here, Dad. Right here, with you."

Chapter One

Missing Moments

THE FARMHOUSE WHERE I GREW UP HAS that sweet musty odor of a century-old wooden home. Ever since I left for college, whenever I came home, it seemed as if the floorboards and walls contained secrets that seeped from each knot in the wood. I used to have a ritual whenever I returned: I would place my hand against the wall next to the front door. When I held my palm there, it was as if I could feel—even see—the various stages of our lives that this house has contained since my sisters and I were small. There is my little sister at age three with her stiff blond hair that grew straight up in the air from the day she was born. There is my older sister strolling by in her bell-bottom blue jeans and Indian print top in high school. There is my mother in what we call The Big Hair Days with her white cat's-eye sunglasses in the 1960s. There is my father, holding his briefcase and wearing a suit as he comes home from work in the 1970s, opening the car door and rubbing the ears of our springer spaniel, who bounded out to the driveway to welcome him.

When I returned at the end of February 2005, there were still a few pine needles stuck in the carpet from Christmas. I remembered what a thrill it had been to come home for the holidays when I had lived in Los Angeles, San Francisco, or New York. Like now, something special would be cooking on the stove. Just as it had happened back then, when I walked in the door, Mom rushed to hug me. But it was different this time, because my father didn't even try to greet me at the door and say hello.

Dad stayed seated in his reclining chair in front of the TV. I could see the back of his big, square head, cocked at an angle I didn't recognize as his. When I walked into the family room, he didn't try to get up. He just shouted, "Who's there?" When my mother said several times "It's our daughter!" he seemed to understand and began to turn his head toward me. After I greeted my mother, I leaned down to the reclining chair to kiss my father's cheek.

This time, instead of feeling the excitement of coming home, what I was experiencing was more like a warm reckoning. This time, instead of settling in for a few days of vacation, knowing I would return to my home in a big city, I had a queasy feeling. Do I belong here? Will I be able to help my father and mother? Will I become the daughter I used to be? Will they treat me like an adult? Will I treat them like the parents they were when I was a teenager? Will our lives expand as we live together, or will our differences make our lives smaller? Will they eventually resent me? Will I resent them?

But the questions seemed to disappear as I hugged my father, and he said, as if I had been away only for a few hours instead of almost twenty years, "I'm so glad you're home."

In the winter of 2005 I moved my luggage, a few books, and my computer up to my room in my parents' house. I had put the rest of my possessions in storage. I sat down on the bed in my tiny room and scanned the corners: there was no place for the things I owned in my former life. The fancy TV I bought in San Francisco and the espresso machine I used every morning before I headed to work would remain in bubble wrap. My beautiful china and glassware and the pots and pans I used when I had friends over for dinner at my apartment in San Francisco would remain in storage, too. There was no room for the trophies and photos of stories I had covered as a journalist over the past twenty years or for my collection of small boxes, my books, my sheet music, my percussion instruments, and my bird identification books. The things that defined me, like much of my life, would remain on hold while I helped my mother take care of my father.

The bedroom was very much like it was when I was little. In fact, I realized as I examined the room that there were no indicators of any of the things I had accomplished since I left home, no sign of the woman I had become. On the shelf in front of the bed were just my Three Little Pigs house, a collection of my Steiff animals, and a few dolls. It was as though my life had remained in suspended animation, my room a museum of the time I had lived there. Everything seemed to have been frozen the day I left for college. Now I would use my mother's china. I would use the furniture I used as a child, and I would try to fit my life into this small bedroom.

I folded the small amount of clothing I had brought with me and put it in drawers. I hung a few suits I used to wear to work in the closet knowing I may not use them for some time. Then I set up my computer in my father's den. His disease has taken away his ability to do anything in there anymore. That's when I started feeling like some sort of interloper. I was moving into some of the spaces he was leaving.

It was a strange feeling, this coming home. I thought I would feel more rooted. But instead I felt *uprooted*. I was stepping into my parents' lives. I didn't have my own life anymore.

A good friend of mine in San Francisco had sent me a card recently with this message: "Sometimes your only available transportation is a leap of faith." It rang very true for me at that point. I had leapt. Had I landed in the right place? I thought the answer was yes. But as with many major life decisions, I had lost some things—and some people—along the way.

For this time in my life, because of this strange and unexpected decision I had made to come home to my parents, I had removed myself from the adrenaline rush and the sometimes cold and ruthless world of reporting and anchoring the news. I was now living my life by totally new rules. Instead of living in the world of broadcast journalism, I was being given a chance to live in a place of total love and caring for someone else.

I didn't have children. Though I had once been married, and though I had had several long-term relationships, my only responsibility in my previous lives in Los Angeles, San Francisco, and New York had been to myself and my career. Trying to have relationships and maintain a high-pressure career at the same time hadn't worked so well. Too often, I simply hadn't given the relationship the time and caring and understanding a relationship needs.

I had never defined myself by a relationship. My work was all that mattered. I handed out business cards wherever I went. I hardly ever introduced myself with just my name. At most social gatherings and appearances, I introduced myself with my name followed by the call letters of the station where I was working at the time: KFWB, KGO, or WCBS Radio. Sometimes friends who were with me on such occasions pointed it out to me and told me it was obnoxious, but I kept doing it anyway. My job at the radio station was who I was.

There are no call letters by my name anymore. Now, for the first time in many, many years, I don't identify myself by my career. My values and priorities and how I think about the world have changed immensely. I define myself and my life in a whole new way. These days, it is the measure of the heart that matters most to me. I can only hope that my heart will be as large as my father's when I begin to leave this world.

"The day he can't tie his tie. That's when you know." That's what one of my mother's friends told her about the moment she knew her husband had Alzheimer's disease. When my mother heard that story, she told me she had thought to herself, That will never happen to me. My father had tied his tie before heading to work every morning for more than forty-five years. His tie (and tying it) was part of his life, part of him. It was how he announced himself to the world. She thought, It will never happen to us. It will never happen to him. And then it did.

My mother says she and my father were heading out to a dinner party. He went into the bathroom to get ready. He spent a very long time inside and then opened the door, holding his tie in his hand with a confused look on his face. He held out the tie and walked up to my mother and said, "Can you help me do this?"

He had forgotten how to tie his tie. My mother says that was a turning point. It's how she knew her life would never be the same, and that my father would never be the same. That was also when she couldn't pretend he didn't have Alzheimer's disease anymore.

Alzheimer's disease is a progressive, irreversible brain disorder with no known cause or cure. It attacks and slowly steals the minds of its victims. At the beginning, symptoms of the disease include memory loss, confusion, impaired judgment, personality changes, disorientation, and loss of language skills. Alzheimer's disease is the most common form of irreversible dementia. It is always fatal.

A German doctor named Dr. Alois Alzheimer discovered the disease a century ago. He noticed changes in the brain tissue of a woman who had died of an unusual mental illness. During an autopsy, he discovered abnormal clumps and tangled bundles of fibers in her brain. Today, these plaques and tangles in the brain are considered signs of Alzheimer's disease. Although scientists are learning more every day, right now they still do not know what causes Alzheimer's.

Though early-onset Alzheimer's can strike people who are

under age sixty, the majority of people are diagnosed in their sixties, seventies, and early eighties. As Alzheimer's takes hold and people lose their memories and abilities, some become angry and violent. Others become docile and childlike. Some, like my father, become even more sweet and gentle than they were before Alzheimer's took hold.

Several decades ago, people with Alzheimer's would simply have been called senile or crazy. They might have been locked away in an insane asylum or nursing home, or left in a wheelchair or hospital bed to atrophy until they died.

Alzheimer's disease attacks the neurons, or nerve cells, in certain areas of the brain, gradually eroding cognitive ability, altering behavior, and affecting a person's ability to live on his or her own. Some people die just a few years after being diagnosed. Some can live twenty years after Alzheimer's symptoms appear. Researchers say the plaques and tangles appear at the same time as a depletion of the neurotransmitters that make up what's called the cholinergic system. This is the system that affects memory and learning. As Alzheimer's disease progresses, this system and the neurons themselves are progressively destroyed. Scientists say that when Alzheimer's kicks in, two significant abnormalities appear in the brain: neurofibrillary tangles, which are twisted nerve cell fibers that appear inside neurons, and neuritic plaques, which are deposits of a sticky protein known as beta amyloid, surrounded by the debris of dying neurons.

As I learned more about my father's disease, I tried to picture the process. So that was it—beta amyloid creeping into my father's brain. This was the enemy. At times I imagined it like some alien substance in a horror film: sticky goo entering his brain, taking my father away.

Researchers have recently been able to identify the spot in the DNA responsible for letting Alzheimer's in. They have pinpointed the place: chromosome 14. I imagine the brightly colored plastic

DNA model from high school displayed on my teacher's desk. It is another target of my rage. That is the place, that is the spot that is responsible for destroying my father's memories. It is why I curse chromosome 14 and beta amyloid on a daily basis.

Here's what doctors and scientists don't tell you about Alzheimer's disease: it breaks your heart a little bit each day. I don't know how my mother, or any spouse who becomes a caregiver for an Alzheimer's victim, survives the pain of caregiving alone.

When I was in New York, I had a vivid recurring dream of my father's head rolling off and falling onto the ground. I wanted so much to stop it and felt, in the dream, that there must be something I could do to keep it from falling. I kept trying to keep his head from hitting the ground, but in the dream there was nothing I could do.

In another dream, my father's face looked normal, the way it used to, before he got Alzheimer's, before his eyes looked slightly vacant, before his face took on a slack, lionlike look. Then his face would crack and fall apart, like it was made of egg-shell-thin porcelain china. In the dream, I would pick up the pieces and try to put his head back together, like in the Humpty-Dumpty nursery rhyme.

When I came back to Michigan, the Humpty-Dumpty dreams stopped. But now there were two new ones. The week after I came home, I dreamed I had Alzheimer's, too. In my dream, everything in my vision seemed to be narrowing and falling away, just the way Dad used to describe his disease to me. ("Everything's escaping," he would say. "Everything's getting smaller.") My vision went from color to black and white and got blurry around the edges. I felt paralyzed and unable to speak. I felt such a profound sense of sorrow, and in the dream, Dad was sad along with me. We said to each other, "We aren't going to be able to tell everyone how much we love them." I felt strongly that I was dying along with my dad.

The dream jarred me awake. When I opened my eyes, I wondered if this was one reason Dad tells us he loves us over and over again. Perhaps he understands that one morning he will wake up and be unable to speak. Or worse, one day he will wake up and he won't know who we are anymore.

The third dream I had after I came home was even more disturbing than the others. In it, Dad was wearing his khaki pants and brown leather jacket. We were in some sort of large store or shopping mall (these are the places where I often worry he will get lost). He looked at his watch repeatedly, the way he often does these days when he's anxious and he feels it's time to go home. In this dream, he looked at his watch one final time, and then he started to run. He ran so fast that I couldn't catch up to him. I tried to stop him, but there was no way I could keep up with him. I had to give up. I simply quit chasing him and watched him disappear. In the dream, I knew he was gone for good. When I woke up, I thought, Maybe Dad is right. Maybe it *is* time for him to go. Maybe we should let him go away on his own. Maybe we're keeping him here longer than he wants to stay.

Recently I found a collection of books about Alzheimer's lined up on a back shelf in the den my father used to use all the time. I picked up one called *Alzheimer's and Dementia.* I thought perhaps these were books my mother had bought after the diagnosis, but when I opened them, I saw they were marked with bright pink magic marker. This isn't Mom's style. She's the one I thought would have been reading this, but I was wrong.

I flipped through the pages. There was Dad's bird-scratching handwriting with his favorite razor-point Pilot pen in the margins. He had apparently bought this book after his diagnosis. I pictured him at his big desk holding that pen of his before he became unable to read, before Alzheimer's took away his ability to comprehend the printed word. He used to spend hours in that room reading and writing letters. He loved corresponding with people and connecting people with others.

But one night, in this very den, he had opened this book not long after his diagnosis and searched for answers about his disease. By the time he read the book I was holding in my hand, he was already losing his ability to spell. He had circled a portion of a paragraph about "adverse reactions" on page 93 and next to it wrote *precicley (sp)* in felt-tip pen. I could tell he had had difficulty trying to remember where the *c*'s and *s*'s should go.

My dad was once a stickler for proper spelling and grammar. In fact, Matt, the man who took over my father's company after he retired, would spend hours putting together presentations on new marketing strategies to help make the company more successful. He would put his presentations in booklets to impress my father, and often, my father would return them with words crossed out, punctuation put in the proper places, and misspelled words corrected. He would then advise Matt to correct the grammar and spelling before he would even discuss the topic of the presentation.

Dad had painstakingly gone through each paragraph of the book on Alzheimer's, underlining furiously, trying to make sense of it, trying to find out what to do. There were lots of exclamation points, lots of yes's in the margins. What could have been going though his mind? Certainly, a kind of fear, and the growing knowledge that his and my mother's lives weren't going to turn out the way they had planned.

More than a decade ago, my father had touched this book trying to find answers. I was now sitting at this same desk, looking through this same book, trying to find answers of my own. Back then, neither of my parents knew the toll it would take on my mother. They probably thought my mother could do this alone. Back then, they didn't know their middle daughter would be coming back home.

I didn't have much time to reflect on this because there was a specific task at hand: getting my father ready for double knee replacement surgery. It was one of the major reasons I had decided to come home. Perhaps this was a good thing because it forced us to dive right into a shared caregiving schedule rather than focusing on how weird it was to be creating this new version of a family.

The first thing my mother and I did was to synchronize our Franklin Planners. Mom filled me in on all the doctor's appointments for the coming weeks. We went through Dad's pills and she described his routine: how he liked his cereal, what was good to give him for lunch, when he should take his pills, when to give him a nutritional supplement, how to get him in the shower and make sure he used his shampoo, how to put out his shaving cream and razor, and how I must stand next to him to make sure he doesn't use the soap instead of the shaving cream. She explained that I would have to show him the toothbrush and make motions with my hands so he would remember how to use it, what channels he likes to watch on TV, what things he can do alone and can't do alone. "Don't let him make a fire alone," she said. "He doesn't understand how to light a match anymore. Don't let him pour beverages for himself anymore; he almost always spills. He doesn't know how to get food for himself anymore." My mother and I were in the process of forming a caregiving team.

As we tried to arrange a daily caregiving schedule, I realized I was writing things such as "pick up Dad's medication" and "call Dad's urologist" in the same columns in my Franklin Planner where I used to write "interview the mayor," "file for ABC News," "staff meeting at KGO," "meet Michaelynn at Café Trieste on Columbus Avenue," "meet Suzie at the San Francisco Symphony," or "meeting today in the WCBS conference room." So much had changed in such a short period of time.

It seemed that we spent the first two weeks either on the phone helping to coordinate the upcoming surgery or going to the doctor. In between, I took my father to a nearby gym to keep his legs strong, following doctor's orders for exercises to get him ready for the upcoming medical procedure.

We started out very organized, focused on the specific task at hand. We filled up each day with activities and appointments, and it seemed we never slowed down until 6 p.m., when we watched the news together. After Dad went to bed, my mother and I read or watched TV or planned the next day together. We were able to talk and get to know each other again. Then, in the night, I would go into my father's den to write.

It was a very different life. I was used to waking up to the sound of a pager or heading to the newsroom to cover a story or anchor the news at 2:30 or 3:30 a.m. for the morning drive show at the radio station, putting in eight- to twelve-hour shifts in the field or in the studio, and then, at night, going out to restaurants and jazz clubs, charity fund-raisers, performances, and shows. When I worked the afternoon anchor shift in New York, I could sleep until 10 a.m. to get to work by noon and could stay out all night long if I wanted to. Life was full of activities, both work-related and social. Lots of parties. Lots of chaos. No particular routine except for my reporting or anchoring shift. It's the way I had always lived. Even if I finally did get to bed at a normal hour, I usually woke up in the middle of the night to write or sing or listen to music. Sometimes I would cook things at odd hours or take a bath at 2 a.m. I have always been restless, and some nights I didn't sleep at all.

I was used to living alone and being as messy as I wanted to be. My older sister says I am dirt blind. This was definitely a problem I was going to have to work on right away. My mother is a perfectionist. She cuts up fresh strawberries in tiny, even, beautiful slices and sprinkles blueberries artfully in my father's and her cereal bowls each morning. When she eats, there are no crumbs at her place. All the surfaces in her kitchen are clean, even when she cooks. The house where we grew up was tidy and orderly most of the time except for the children's bedrooms.

My life in Los Angeles, San Francisco, and New York was the complete opposite. My bedroom was a tornado of clothes and piles of dirty laundry. In the kitchen, dirty dishes might sit for days on counters or in the sink while I worked on a big story. I didn't care. I felt I didn't have to. I lived alone. Though I love to cook, the rest of domestic life has always eluded me. Through the years, I had hired several cleaning teams to help me out, and several of them had simply disappeared or quit. My neighbor saw one of the people I hired running from my apartment with the cord of her vacuum trailing behind her. There was, he said, a look of panic and anger in her eyes. I never saw her again.

When I got around to it, I usually took my laundry to a service down the street. I didn't even know how to iron and didn't have the patience to mend anything. Once, when I was covering a story in Los Angeles, a button fell off the front of my shirt in a very revealing spot. I was going live on a story every twenty minutes and had no time to sew on a button (nor the knowledge or talent to do so) and had no safety pin with me. I walked into a Gap store and in lightning speed picked out and bought a new shirt. I changed in the dressing room. I took the shirt with the missing button out on the street and gave it to a homeless person. Then I picked up the microphone and continued reporting live on the story I was covering.

My mother would never throw a shirt away just because of a missing button. She is a child of the Depression. That would be considered a terrible waste. Besides, she probably could have sewn on the button in a matter of seconds.

She has all sorts of mysterious, sweet-smelling laundry-, sewing-, and ironing-related products. She once told me she actually takes pleasure in ironing my father's shirts. She mended and even sewed some of our clothes. She darned socks. For me, these things were almost unimaginable.

Now that I had come home, she was teaching me about alien

procedures and products that I'd never learned or cared about before. For instance, she explained that Soft Scrub with Bleach is the only way to clean a kitchen sink. Linoleum simply doesn't shine without Mop & Glo. And Oxyclean—it cleans everything. How did I live without it?

Basically, I was messy. Extremely messy. And disorganized. So the living arrangement of the three of us was going to be a challenge. My mother, a clean, organized perfectionist, was now living with a woman who had no desire to keep house and a man who couldn't remember how.

When I first came home, I worked on learning how to clean up after myself and not leave dishes and pots and pans out when I cooked. I vowed to try to keep communal areas as clean as possible. Mom vowed to not even venture upstairs to look at the way I conducted my life in my childhood bedroom and the room next to it I was using as a sort of office. It was a hands-off, sight-unseen rule, kind of like a domestic "don't ask, don't tell" policy to protect my mother's mental health.

Because laundry was not my specialty, my mother volunteered to continue being the laundress for all three of us, promising no resentment for her role. We have dubbed her "laundry queen" because she is so good at it. She says it gives her satisfaction. Perhaps it's because when you live with someone who has Alzheimer's, you can never be finished with anything. But laundry? Laundry you can thoroughly clean. You can finish it and fold it and put it away in drawers and say when it's done, unlike my father's Alzheimer's, which is always unraveling and out of control.

What struck me most when I came home was that everything was so quiet. At times a whole day would go by with only the sound of a few trucks going by on our dirt road or a barking dog. Deer often graze in our backyard. I was used to the sounds of sirens and car horns in L.A., San Francisco, or New York, cell phones and pagers going off constantly. But the only loud noise I could recall after coming home was when a flock of wild turkeys pecked against the windows in the family room one morning.

No matter how hard I tried to live my life in a cleaner, quieter, and more organized fashion, however, I still brought some of my frenetic life with me to this quiet house in the country and into my parents' lives. I was transferring my passion for reporting to a passion for taking care of my father and helping my mother. I thought that I would dive right into the task of caregiving the way I dove into a big story. I suppose I figured that if I attacked the task this way, there wouldn't be much time to have regrets about this new life I had taken on.

I saw my job as threefold. First, I wanted to help my mother take care of my father by taking on some of the routine caregiving duties so she could try to have her own life. I saw this not just as helping with the quality of her life, but also as a way to actually help prolong her life, to free her of the shackles of defining herself as Dad's sole caregiver and help her see there could be a future of her own, another chapter in her life in which she could do many of the things that she had been unable to do while she was taking care of Dad alone.

Second, I saw myself as a kind of companion for my father, to help ease the emotional burden for my mother and to make my father feel more comfortable. I wanted to help my mother take care of Dad by buying groceries, fixing some of his food, taking him to some of his doctor's appointments, taking care of him alone both in and outside of the home so Mom could do things on her own, and begin to take him to day care on a regular basis. I also wanted to create a relationship with him separate from his relationship with my mother so that he could become less dependent on her. Physical and mental exercises, including singing songs, became part of our routine. I wanted to create daily rituals that were our own so my mother wouldn't be the only one responsible for his well-being. And I wanted to help with the daily housework (even though it was, as yet, foreign to me) that my dad couldn't understand how to do anymore in order to ease the physical burden for my mother.

Third, I saw myself as someone who could help execute not only routine and mundane activities but fun and relaxing things, everything from getting my mother out the door to get a manicure and pedicure to getting her to go on a Caribbean cruise—in other words, to help my mother not only have her own life but also to begin actually enjoying life again.

These were the things I wanted to accomplish. I set out to do them the way I would approach any big story. Of course, I wanted to succeed. I was used to winning awards and getting the big stories and getting answers to my questions and being on the number one show. What I didn't know at the time is that you can't win at caregiving. You can't succeed. You can only help a little bit along the way. But, as I would learn later, that doesn't necessarily mean you have failed.

Chapter Two

The Big Decline

FOR FOUR DECADES, MY FATHER WAS CEO of E and E Engineering in Detroit, an industrial distribution firm. He took great pride in knowing every detail about the equipment he sold to the "Big Three" automakers and other companies across the United States. But he took just as much pride in knowing everything he could about the sixty people who worked for him. He could recall details of the lives of the people he dealt with on a daily basis: not just the presidents of GM, Ford, and Chrysler, but also the men who worked on the assembly line or a salesperson he met on the road. He remembered their hobbies; what colleges they had attended; their wives', children's, and husbands' names; even what kind of pet they had (this was partly because he had owned several springer spaniels he adored, and he felt you could tell a lot about people by what kinds of pets they chose). Today he can't recall the names of members of his own family. He can't remember what happened ten minutes ago. Alzheimer's has taken his past away.

People said that when they spoke with my father, they often felt they were the only one in the room. When he walked into social gatherings, people who knew him shouted his name and approached him heartily with handshakes and hugs. He entered into long, intimate conversations with people everywhere he went—on planes, trains, and golf courses, in jazz clubs and restaurants. For my father, potential friends were around every corner. He took detailed notes about the people he met; he wrote their addresses and phone numbers on three-by-five cards, which he placed in his upper left suit coat pocket. Then he connected them with other people he thought they might enjoy. He helped hundreds of people get jobs by introducing them to people he had met on the road. He kept up correspondences (with large handwriting in felt-tip pen on his blue E and E Engineering stationery) with all these people for years and often became close friends, visiting them when he'd pass through their towns.

My father has always been an optimist—to a fault. He believed the best about people to the point that some people thought of him as naïve. He helped others whenever he could, loaning money to people who never paid him back. I talked with him about this tendency on several occasions, and his answer was always the same: "If they need it that badly, I'm glad to help." Sometimes I would tell him that I thought he might have been ripped off. Again, a consistent answer: "I would rather have it be that way than the other way around."

As you might imagine, my father's optimism about humankind could be especially frustrating for people who were close to him, like my mother. There was the time my mother had surgery to have a benign tumor removed from her brain. I was with my mother and father as she was being wheeled into the operating room. The anesthetics were already kicking in. My mother was wearing a blue surgery cap. My father, holding her hand as an attendant wheeled her down the hall, looked into her eyes as he repeated the words "Isn't it wonderful?" over and over again. I saw Mom's eyes begin to narrow. That was when I started to realize how difficult it might be at times to live with my overly optimistic father. I hoped the anesthetics had kicked in enough that she wouldn't remember those last words before she entered the operating room.

My father's calendars and letters from the 1970s tell the story of a man who was CEO of a successful industrial distribution company, developed his own manufacturing plant, served on the strategic planning committee of the city of Detroit and on the Detroit economic development committee, served on the board of Detroit's Warren/Connor urban development group, rehearsed and performed on a weekly basis as baritone in a twelve-man a cappella singing group, sang and rehearsed each week with the church choir, golfed regularly at the Detroit Golf Club, was a jazz aficionado, was an active supporter of the University of Michigan alumni association, performed with a community theater group called the Avon Players, and was a card-carrying member of the International Frisbee Association who was known to fling Frisbees on a regular basis. He still got home most nights to see his "four girls"—my mother, my older sister, Alison, my little sister, Libby, and me. And of course, the springer spaniel, Happy Dingleflopper.

We adored him. My mother always made sure she was perfectly coiffed as 7 p.m. drew near. When we were small, we dressed up and put ribbons in our hair before dinnertime so we'd look nice when my father walked in the door. I still remember the sound of the tires of his big car crunching on the gravel in the driveway when he came home from work. One of us would shout "Dad's home!" and we'd run to greet him. When we took ballet, we appeared at the door wearing our pink tutus and did a pirouette or two to welcome him home.

My father, with his Kent cigarettes and wingtips, burst into song at a moment's notice. In the 1960s, he looked like Dick Van Dyke in his gray suit and thin tie. When he came home from work, if Stan Kenton or Frank Sinatra was on the stereo, he would take my mother in his arms, swirl her through the kitchen, and swing her across the linoleum as though it were a fancy ballroom floor. He can still wrap his arms around my mother and twirl her across the dance floor the way he did when they met in college. But these days he is doing another kind of dance, too—a dance through the labyrinth in his brain that is Alzheimer's.

• • •

For everyone who loves someone with Alzheimer's, there are markers and moments that tell you the disease is on the way. Sometimes, you look these indicators in the eye. Other times, you simply turn away. It is possible that my family and I blocked out many of the moments that might have signaled Alzheimer's was already invading my father's brain. A few moments, in retrospect, were turning points.

My mother recalls a winter night (years ago now) when she and my father went to see a play with two other couples. My father volunteered to drive everyone from the town where they live in the suburbs about twenty miles north of the city to the theater in downtown Detroit. Dad dropped all five of them off at the entrance to the theater and then went to park the car alone. When they came outside after the performance, Dad had absolutely no idea where he had parked the car. Nothing. No recollection or even a clue as to what direction he might have walked from, or the name of the parking garage. The group of friends wound up wandering around through unsafe areas in downtown Detroit in the freezing cold for more than an hour until they finally discovered Dad's car.

My father started getting lost when he drove to places that had been routine in his life—places he'd driven to for years. Then the most frightening moments, when my mother knew something was wrong: Dad couldn't remember entire events, such as dinners, parties, trips, and musical performances they'd attended the night before. Yet, for quite some time, my mother says she simply covered up for him, telling him—and telling herself—that this was just a phase.

She says she knew it was time to go the doctor when names of common objects started disappearing from his vocabulary and when he started being unable to find certain rooms in the house. My mother would ask my father to take some clothes to the laundry room and he would appear a few moments later holding the bundle she had given to him in his hands and say, "Where's the laundry room?" Groceries he had helped my mother put away wound up in strange places. Then he started forgetting people's names, even the names of people that he'd known for thirty years who were in his singing group. Finally, events in his past and the names of relatives were lost entirely.

My mother and my sisters don't seem to remember exactly when and how we knew, though the signs had been there for a couple of years. No one wanted to talk about it, until finally my family was gathered for the New Year's holiday at my little sister Libby's house in West Virginia. I was in San Francisco. At some point, my mother said to my sisters, "Your father is having memory problems," and Alison, my older sister, said, "I was wondering when you were going to talk with us about it."

The more my mother told people about her concerns, the more she realized that almost everyone who spent time with my father suspected he had Alzheimer's, too. That's when she decided it was time to go to a specialist.

One of the most shocking moments for my mother, she says, is when the doctor began casually asking my father questions that seemed to be routine, things one ought to know in one's daily life. She thought this part of their appointment would be the least difficult, but when the doctor pointed to the watch on his wrist and asked my father to name it, my father could not recall the word *watch*. My mother says she was stunned. She said she had no idea it had reached this point; they had been trying to live their lives in a normal fashion, covering up for his memory problems for so long. Then the doctor held up the pen he was using and asked my father to identify it. Nothing. My father turned to my mother, searching for the word. She says a look of panic appeared in his eyes. She didn't mouth the word for him this time.

At the time my father was being diagnosed with Alzheimer's, he heard about clinical trials in an advertisement on the radio. Volunteers were needed for a University of Michigan–affiliated study. At first my mother was wary of responding to any sort of advertisement, in broadcast or in print, involving medical treatment. But they both checked it out, asked questions, felt it was a reputable clinic, and decided to take the risk. That's when they met the man who became my father's geriatric psychiatrist, Dr. Stephen Aronson. He began concocting a cocktail of medicines and "talk therapy" to try to give my father the best chance to live his life as normally as possible with Alzheimer's, and to slow down the deadly effects of the disease as long as possible.

Yet even though they had caught the disease quite early, in as little as one year after the diagnosis, traveling to the store, much less overseas, started getting difficult. My mother seemed to be doing triage at every turn.

As we would learn in the coming years, to continue living "normally" with an Alzheimer's patient means that the spouse—in this case, my mother—does the brunt of the work and becomes physically and emotionally exhausted. It is quite often the survival of the caregiver that begins to hang in the balance, and the caregiver's health becomes more precarious than that of the person living with Alzheimer's.

The combination of my father's overoptimism and his incredible penchant for denial (a family trait) helped us pretend that he wasn't diagnosed with a fatal brain disease longer than many families might be able to. Every day there was less my father could do, and more my mother was forced to do: paying the bills, doing the taxes, managing the finances, doing the yard work, taking care of all household chores—all the things one must do to keep a home going, because Dad couldn't remember how to do them anymore. In addition to all that, eventually she had to tell my father, each morning, where his underwear was, and where *he* was, and what a toothbrush was, and how to use it. It was the beginning of the Big Decline.

Families are often forced to admit what's happening when they realize they are putting their lives and other people's lives in danger by letting the Alzheimer's patient continue to drive. My sisters started getting nervous about their children riding in the car when my father was at the wheel. When he began to believe it was all right to drive down the middle of the street with the white line centered between the two front tires ("I've seen truck drivers do it," Dad said. "I only do it when other cars aren't around," and, "It helps me keep my options open, whether I want to turn left or right"), we knew we couldn't let Dad drive anymore. But of course, none of us helped Mom close that door.

He started blowing through stop signs. My mother said every time she rode with him, she had to make sure he saw pedestrians and bike riders. My mother just started taking the wheel, more and more. He would head toward the driver's seat, but she would simply step ahead of him and say, "Why don't you let me drive? You've driven all your life." As always, my mother came up with a graceful response to a less than graceful event in their lives.

At first, it was difficult for my father to acquiesce and let Mom take control of the car. The automobile was a symbol of his identity and masculinity for the majority of his life (my mother says he told her once, "It makes me feel like a man to drive"). But after he got lost trying to get home alone from Detroit and couldn't even tell the people at the gas station who were trying to help him where he lived, even he began to know it was time to let go of the wheel. Once my mother became the person who drove, my father grew more passive. Mom and Dad stopped going to parties and traveling as much as they had before.

My mother was becoming more and more exhausted. My sisters, my mother, and I finally started to talk about what to do next. One thing we knew for sure was that a nursing home wasn't an option for us at this point. We had watched our grandparents spend their last years there, and we didn't like it. My maternal grandmother died alone in a nursing home. It was a horrible existence. She hated it and had even tried to escape. Toward the end of her life, she couldn't speak. She was strapped into a wheelchair and drugged. The experience devastated my mother. None of us will ever forgive ourselves for allowing that to happen. My paternal grandmother died in the nursing home she had lived in for nine years. Though my mother and father were by her side when she died, her life in those final years was dismal and depressing.

When my mother's sister was diagnosed with inoperable cancer, my mother flew to Seattle to be by her side. She stayed with Aunt Beth for quite some time and was able to hold her hand not long before she died. My mother said she felt my aunt could sense the love in the room as she exited this world. I remember vividly that when she came back home to Michigan, my mother told me on the phone, "Please have someone I love be with me to hold my hand when I die. It's so important."

My parents made a pact then to try to never end up in a nursing home. They started studying about the Hemlock Society. They stock-piled pills. They made jokes about Jack Kevorkian. They told each other that in the case of a fatal disease, they'd help each other decide how and when to leave this world. But they didn't take into account the in-between world that is Alzheimer's. They didn't take into account the fact that one of them might not be able to make a choice.

As Dad's Alzheimer's got worse, I asked my mother about getting someone to come to the house to take care of my father. It was immediately clear that the idea of a stranger living with them was unacceptable to my mother. She had heard too many tales of stolen items, stolen privacy, a stolen life. For my mother, having a person live in the home to help take care of Dad symbolized "the end of life as she knew it." It was a definite sign of failure. It wasn't an option, at least not yet.

We discussed the idea of Mom and Dad moving to be near one of us. My older sister, Alison, runs the Service Learning Program and teaches public health courses at Kalamazoo College, a private liberal arts institution in western Michigan. Her husband is a professor at the same college. They own a home in Kalamazoo and are raising a teenage son. Kalamazoo is about four hours away from my parents' home. Moving Mom and Dad to Kalamazoo was an option.

My younger sister, Libby, is an editor with two sons and a husband and a sprawling house on a hill in a small town in West Virginia she has called home for more than twenty years. A move to West Virginia? My parents don't know anyone there except my sister and her family, and it's very far away from their summer home on a northern Michigan lake. It wasn't likely.

I lived in a one-bedroom apartment on Telegraph Hill in San Francisco. Could they consider moving to the Bay Area to an assisted living facility or a condo? My mother couldn't imagine it. She loves the woods and lakes of Michigan, and besides, the cost of living in the Bay Area made the move impractical.

Finally it came down to this question: could my parents leave the home in the country where they had lived for more than fifty years, the home where all three of us were raised? My mother said she couldn't fathom turning the key in the lock in the front door for the last time. No way. Besides, my father was already getting disoriented in his own home. My mother decided that moving from the family home would be bad for both of them, and the doctors treating my father concurred.

Then we thought, Could one of us move in with my parents? As it is for many women these days, my sisters' time was consumed with children and careers. Moving back home for even a short period would have been financially and emotionally risky for either of them and their families. That's when what seemed like a large arrow appeared over my head. (My parents didn't put the arrow there; I did.) I didn't have a husband. I didn't have children. I didn't own a home. I spoke to millions of people each week as I broadcast on the ABC radio station in San Francisco, but I didn't even own a plant or a pet. I had had a failed marriage long ago. I was living what appeared to be a "single life," though I was in an ongoing long-distance relationship with a man who lived in New York.

Meanwhile, my father's disease was progressing. I could hear the exhaustion and depression in my mother's voice on the phone. I invited my parents out to San Francisco for the Associated Press Reporter of the Year awards ceremony to help celebrate an accolade I felt I had worked very hard to earn. They couldn't fly out to celebrate with me, she said. Everything had simply become too difficult to do with Dad, especially travel.

I remember in that moment wondering what we, as a family, were going to do about my father's disease. We had no plan, and my mother's and father's lives were spiraling downward. My mother was now at risk of losing her own life in the process of trying to keep my father out of a nursing home.

My mother, Rosemary, is graceful and strong. She's an artist, an educator, and an intellectual. She was an art major at the University of Michigan and went on to teach at several public schools. When my sisters and I were little, she made a deal with the principal of a private school we attended not far from our home: if she taught art there, we could get free tuition.

Like my father, she multitasked before it was popular. She not only taught art at the elementary school we attended, but also made a beautiful home for us, complete with homemade dinners almost every night. She painted and made block prints, illustrated several books, sewed dresses for us (and ironed our hair ribbons!), ran several charity organizations, and wound up pursuing a master's degree at Oakland University.

It is only lately that I have come to realize that my mother's competence has worked against her. When you do everything so well, it's extremely difficult to ask for help, and it's extremely difficult for the people who love you to believe you *need* help. What's worse, when you appear that competent and successful, you get no training in how to tell other people you need them. Desperately. Even your own children.

After my father's diagnosis, my sisters and I tried to visit my parents more often. Fortunately, my sisters could spend a large amount of time in the summer months at my parents' cottage with the three grandchildren in tow. For the summer, my mother had my sisters, the grandchildren, and brothers-in-law to help not only with my father's care but also with cooking and cleaning. They filled up the empty spaces for my parents. My father came alive with the children and grandchildren around. I would fly in from San Francisco for two weeks in July or August, and during that time, the whole family would be together to surround my father and help with caregiving, grocery shopping, making dinner, and doing household chores. We had bonfires and big family meals; one of us would play tennis, play Frisbee, or go swimming with Dad almost every day. The presence of family members not only to take care of Dad but also to cushion the blow of the loss of my father to Alzheimer's (so glaringly apparent when a husband and wife live alone) helped my mother survive the first decade of my father's disease.

Summers seemed to sustain my parents in so many ways. Summer buoyed them up, before the season began and after it ended. Planning for it kept them busy and distracted, and they were sustained by the memory of it after it was over.

There was the family, filling up every room of the cottage on the lake. There were the grandchildren, paddling the canoe or setting out in the sailboat. Each summer, when I came home, I would see my mother and father hold hands as they sat on the porch, watching the grandchildren diving into and climbing out of the water the way our grandparents had seen us play in Walloon Lake. We'd bundle up in blankets, all ten of us sometimes, including the "granddog," the golden retriever, and watch falling stars together on the dock. We'd make peppermint tea from the plants we picked along the shore. Even when Alzheimer's started setting in, Dad would come with us and nestle in a sleeping bag on the dock. After watching the Perseid meteor shower, we'd toddle off to bed.

But at the end of every summer, there'd come the days when the mornings would get colder. Red and yellow leaves began to drift down into the mirror surface of the lake, signaling it was time to go. The families packed up, and the kids went back to school.

After my father got Alzheimer's, when fall rolled around, my mother was left alone with Dad to close up the summer cottage and move back to their year-round home near Detroit. Closing up the cottage was a particularly difficult task with someone who had Alzheimer's. My mother says that as his disease set in, the move up north and back became exhausting partly because my father became unable to visualize anything. He couldn't help out with a simple task such as handing Mom a box or moving a chair because he couldn't tell what a box or a chair was anymore. Everything took twice as long to accomplish. Eventually, as happens with many Alzheimer's patients and their caregivers as the disease progresses, it became easier to simply not include him in many tasks.

Mom became overworked. My father, on the other hand, felt useless. Each year, as my father's disease got worse, the return to their lives near Detroit was more difficult—packing, unpacking, cleaning, moving things from up north back home. A pervasive depression seemed to settle in for both of them. The reality of the disease had finally kicked in, and the exhaustion of taking care of an Alzheimer's patient alone and running not one but two homes began sapping my mother's life away. I called and came home as much as I could, as did both of my sisters while they continued the difficult task of balancing jobs and children.

As my father's disease got worse, my career seemed to be taking off. It was odd, this juxtaposition. I became the morning drive reporter at the top news station in Los Angeles and drove throughout southern California speeding to stories, studying maps of the area, learning to work radio equipment, and broadcasting live every twenty minutes.

My father started getting lost driving home from various familiar spots in Detroit.

I went live nationwide reporting on the L.A. riots.

My father couldn't remember what a refrigerator was.

More murders, more fires. My friends started calling me Danger Girl. I began doing investigative reports and working for the network more and more.

My father forgot the names of his own mother and brother.

The ABC News station in San Francisco hired me and I made the move from L.A. to the Bay Area.

My father got lost while driving to the corner grocery store, to the neighbors', and to a friend's home where he has visited frequently for more than two decades.

I covered the O.J. Simpson trial for ABC News.

My father could no longer remember the names of the people he had worked with for thirty years.

An earthquake hit the Bay Area, and I went live on the network for several hours.

My mother and father decided they simply couldn't travel overseas anymore.

I was sent to London to cover the death of Princess Diana for KGO Radio and ABC News.

My family decided it wasn't safe for my father to drive anymore.

I became morning anchor at the number one radio station in San Francisco.

My mother began having difficulty facing my father's disease or taking him to day care or even contemplating getting someone into our home.

Our morning show won several awards for being the best in the Bay Area.

My father began repeating questions over and over again, hanging his head as he sat in a chair, and saying he wanted to die. My mother began saying she sometimes felt that way, too.

I won the Associated Press Reporter of the Year award.

My father could no longer read, and the only thing he seemed to be able to write anymore was his name. He couldn't remember how to put on his shoes or tie his tie. My parents were finding it difficult to go to the symphony or even to see their friends. They hardly went out anymore.

I got hired as an anchor at a top-rated radio station in New York. I talked to millions of people each day. But it didn't matter anymore. I only wanted to talk to two: my father and my mother.

One Sunday afternoon when I was visiting my parents for the weekend, a few hours before my flight back to New York, I said, "Dad, let's go on a walk." It was autumn, and brilliantly colored leaves lined the country road. I told him to put on his coat and meet me outside.

I didn't realize until we got out to the road that he had put on my mother's powder-blue jacket instead of his own. The sleeves were much too short. He looked like a child who had suddenly grown too big for his clothes. We were on the road, walking together, when he said, once again, "Why do you have to leave? Why can't you stay here with us?" Because the coat was much too small to zip up over his large body, he ran his hands up and down the useless zipper clasp in the nervous-tick way he has developed since he got Alzheimer's. Then he looked down at the powder-blue jacket only partially covering his stomach, the sleeves coming only halfway down his arms, and looked embarrassed as he said, "I have your mother's coat on, don't I?" I started to cry, the kind of crying that just won't stop. I knew then that I wanted to come home to help Mom make sure Dad didn't accidentally wear someone else's clothes when he walked out on the road. I wanted to come home to help make sure his hair was combed properly. I wanted to help Mom make sure that the doctors and nurses who treated him were giving him the care he needed. I wanted to help Mom make sure he took the right combination of pills each morning and evening.

I wanted to come home to have the time to say good-bye.

Chapter Three

A Rainbow Might Appear

ONE NIGHT AFTER I HAD BEEN HOME for several weeks, I made a chicken salad sandwich for Dad and placed it in front of him at his usual place at the table. He stared at it for a while in what I have come to understand is a time of processing. These days, rather than explaining what's in front of him, and how to eat it, we simply wait for him to figure out what to do with it. We intervene only when necessary. It's better for him and for us, and it cuts down on the stress at mealtimes.

It's very different from the way it used to be. Before I moved back home, after my father was several years into the disease, he would stare at the plate in front of him and say, "It's too much!" or, "It's too big." Then he would say, "I'm not hungry" followed by, "I can't eat that." Meals became a whine session, with my father complaining and not being able to grasp how to eat the food or simply not eating the food at all, followed by my mother or my sisters or me trying to coax him to eat while we showed him what utensils to use and how to eat the food in front of him. The entire process was depressing.

Fortunately, after I came home, we discovered the book *Learning to Speak Alzheimer's* by Joanne Koenig Coste. In it, Koenig Coste explains the way the disease affects depth perception and perception of colors, and the way this can affect mealtime and many other activities. For instance, if you serve white cauliflower and white fish and white potatoes on a white plate, the Alzheimer's patient may not eat it because he simply can't see it. He can't process what's in front of him. On the other hand, a plate filled with lots of colors and different textures and kinds of food causes a feeling of chaos in many Alzheimer's patients. They often won't eat a full plate of different types of foods because they simply can't figure out what to do with each item. It's a problem Koenig Coste says nursing homes and hospitals have only recently begun addressing.

Koenig Coste suggests putting only one or two types of food of different colors on each plate and serving finger foods and simple items that don't require utensils. Nancy Mace and Peter Rabin also make these suggestions in their handbook for caregivers of Alzheimer's patients titled *The 36-Hour Day*. We took the advice from both of these books, and the results were amazing.

We started giving Dad more sandwiches and finger foods, and we stopped ordering large plates of food filled with different items when we went out to restaurants. These small changes made life easier for all of us, and Dad's appetite improved. Now, rather than explaining things on his plate, or trying to get him to eat right away, or coaxing him to use a fork or spoon, we just wait to see if he will begin to understand what's in front of him, whether it's a sandwich, finger food, or something that needs utensils. Most of the time he figures it out eventually. If he doesn't, why not let him eat with his hands, or even use the wrong utensil, especially if we're at home?

Getting an Alzheimer's patient to do things the way people who are not impaired do them is, in many cases, stressful for both the patient and the caregiver and could actually do more harm than good for both. Is it so important that he act like a "normal" person? To me, it's not. But it may be to others, especially when we are in public. So we do the necessary dance when we go out to restaurants, the dance of making sure he's using the proper utensils and eating his food properly, because, I suppose, it makes people around us more comfortable.

As we learned with the alterations in mealtime rituals, it is easier to actually change to Dad's way of being—to what's easier for and makes sense to Dad—than to make *him* adjust to *us* and to our non-Alzheimer's world. Nowhere is this more apparent than in the world of language.

So now we go back to the chicken salad sandwich I made for Dad that day. He figured out on his own that it was a sandwich and that it was something that he could pick up with his hands. He maneuvered the sandwich into his mouth and took a bite. Pieces of it fell onto the plate. He asked, "Can I have a handle to work on this?" "Sure, Dad," I said and handed him a fork. That's when I realized I was using *his* language now. In fact, it *is* a handle, in a way. In this instance, the word fits. That isn't always the case.

Sometimes the words Dad uses are creative new explanations of objects or ideas. Sometimes, though, words are complete reversals of what they once were. Lately, he points to an object, and the word for it simply isn't there. It's gone.

From what I have heard from other caregivers and from the books I've read about Alzheimer's, the use of language is one of the first indications that Alzheimer's is setting in. Sometimes the words are flipped around. Sometimes the patient can't find the word. And sometimes there are wonderful new ways the Alzheimer's patient refers to objects.

My father has been calling the TV "the radio" for several years now. No one who spends time with him corrects him anymore. We simply know what he is referring to when he wants to watch the television, and we get out the remote when he begins obsessively wanting "the radio." Maybe, because my career has been in radio for so many years, I secretly like it that he thinks the TV is the radio.

Once, he called me in a very upset tone from his bedroom. "Daughter, can you help me with this?" He was in front of the TV with the remote in his hands. "Look at the radio!" he said in a shocked tone. It was a horrible TV picture—hardly decipherable, snowy black-and-white dots instead of the show he wanted to watch.

"Can you fix this?" he asked. "It's all . . . trinkley!" I thought, you know, it *is* trinkley! It's a very good word for what happens when the picture on your TV screen gets messed up.

When you spend time with a person living with Alzheimer's, you learn that certain key words mean something else. For instance, Dad's wallet and his keys are of paramount importance to him. As Alzheimer's takes hold of his brain, those three words have become interchangeable. Sometimes, the word *car* gets in the mix, too. My family has a theory that all those things mean independence and power and success, and that is why they are lumped in the same category in my father's brain. The people who spend the most time with my father simply realize this, and there is no need to correct him. When he's anxious and looking around for something, we just show him where all those things are. Then he's calm and relieved. His anxiety dissipates.

The other day, my father and I were in my car. He performed what has become a daily ritual of patting his breast pocket and then his pants pocket. This is what he does when he searches for his wallet. "Where's the car?" he said. I answered, "It's in your pocket, Dad." He patted his pants pocket, feeling the outline of his leather wallet. He nodded and said, "Yes, there it is!" I realized then that I was adopting his vernacular, I was understanding and using *his* words instead of trying to teach him mine. I've come to believe that's the way it should be, in many cases. There is no need to correct him all the time. So, for now, for today, the car is in his pocket, and that's fine with both of us.

In the car, we sometimes sing songs together. Although he has replaced so many words with other ones when he uses normal language, when he sings a song, almost every lyric—and every single note—is perfect.

When I was a little girl, my parents, both graduates of the University of Michigan, used dinnertime not only to catch up on their

own and their children's lives but also to educate us. My father kept
a globe, an atlas, and a dictionary right next to his place at the dinner
table so we could look up words, countries, and states—and resolve
arguments before they came to blows. He taught junior high school
math and science after graduating from college. He decided not to
pursue a career in teaching, however, and chose industry instead.

At dinner, though, the teacher in my father would always re-
emerge. Dad liked to ask us questions about our extracurricular
activities and our classes, but often swayed the conversation toward
geography. Sometimes he would test us on the names of state capi-
tals. He had memorized every single one.

As the plaque builds up in his brain and there is less and less
for us to do together and talk about, I keep trying to come up with
new ideas for activities, things that will connect his old life with
this one, as he slowly slips away.

I thought puzzles might be the way to go. I bought a wooden
puzzle of the United States. Each piece was in the shape of a state
with the capital listed on the puzzle piece. I thought it would be
perfect for us to do together and maybe provide something for us
to talk about as we did the task. But when we began, I realized he
didn't remember what a state was, and the concept of putting a
puzzle piece in its proper spot was completely alien to him. I tried
to explain, but it didn't work. I resorted to sneaking the proper
puzzle piece next to him and suggesting a spot for him to put it.
"There!" he would exclaim when South Dakota slid into the
proper opening. But he didn't recall enough about the process to
begin doing it again, to initiate the act of picking up a piece and
searching for another place to fit it in. After each puzzle piece
clicked in place, I had to explain how to do it all over again. It was
clear he didn't really understand. Together, we put the pieces in
their designated spots, but I grew sadder with each moment,
watching the father who used to teach me so many things, unable
to conceive of where a state was, or even *what* it was.

Sometimes, your wonderful idea of how to help an Alzheimer's patient participate in the world doesn't work. In fact, sometimes you have to admit that the idea is more for *you*, to help you pretend he's the person he was before the disease took hold.

I learned a lesson with the puzzle. In fact, after an exasperating half hour, I finally asked Dad if he liked doing the puzzle with me. "Not really," he said. I realized that a lot of what he might be doing throughout each day is humoring us, and not the other way around! Sometimes you just have to scratch all your plans and start over.

Despite the daily frustrations of learning how to help my mother take care of a person living with Alzheimer's, at the beginning, it was a pleasure to be home. My parents and I visited familiar places from my childhood. We took long drives on country roads where I used to go to school. It was wonderful to have time to just talk and be with my mother and get to know more about her. I felt as though I were visiting a part of life I had missed for the twenty years I had been pursuing my career, the domestic part. Shopping and cooking food for Mom and Dad and me (instead of being home alone and cooking for one) was a great pleasure for me. We even had several dinner parties with some old friends of my parents. We did lots of activities that were too difficult for Mom to do with Dad alone, such as going to the symphony and museums.

Mom seemed relieved to have some company in the laborious routines of the day and to simply have someone there to watch over Dad and help clothe him, give him his pills, feed him, and make sure he was comfortable. Dad seemed happy to have my company. He repeated often, in the morning, to my mother, "Is our daughter here?" She said he seemed pleased each morning to know that there was someone new to hang out with and that the two of them weren't alone. He continued to repeat throughout the day, "Daughter, where are you?" I would answer, "Here I am," and he would always say, "I'm so glad you're here."

A friend of mine, whose sister is in a situation like mine, calls it The Beloved Dysfunctional Triad. That describes my father and mother and me, too, trying to work out a way to be together in our new roles. At times we weren't clear about who was supposed to perform certain tasks. It was almost as if some sort of synchronized mothering instinct would kick in. One day we both brought him a glass of chocolate milk at the same time. Sometimes we arrived with a Coke or Ensure to give to him and almost ran into each other exiting the kitchen. At first, I probably took over too many things and got in my mother's way. Then there were times I am sure I didn't do enough.

Another time, on a day when Dad seemed very down, my mother and I didn't check in with each other very much as we did paperwork or other errands in the house. Dad started to act rather strangely and seemed dizzy. When we sat down to lunch, he seemed loopy and odd and kept saying how tired he was. He seemed particularly sensitive to noise. We discussed how strange he seemed, and then we both blurted at the same time, "I gave him some Marinol" (it's a legal derivative of marijuana we had obtained from his G.P. to help his appetite and his mood). Uh-oh. We had both given him a dose of a potentially hallucinogenic drug! In other words, he was overdosing on Marinol and was probably experiencing a kind of marijuana high! He kept saying he was dizzy and, as I recall, he had to have a nap. I felt bad about that one.

After the Marinol incident, we made sure to tell each other when we gave him his pills. Even so, I recently accidentally gave him his morning pills in the evening, and Mom didn't know it, so she woke him up after he'd already gone to bed and gave him his evening pills. It could have been a bad mix of things. But even though he had double doses of some pills, and was given some of his morning pills at night, he slept extremely well and didn't seem to have any ill effects from our mistake. So the days went by after I came home—trying new things, failing, scratching plans, making mistakes, and starting all over again.

Dad and I drove around in the car a lot listening to music and singing songs together. That seemed to be one of his favorite things to do. We went to the gym as much as possible. It was what the doctor had advised, and my father seemed to enjoy it. This also gave my mother time alone to hopefully remember what it was like to have her own life. While my father and I were together, I could begin the process of reconnecting with him and come up with new ways to keep him occupied and stimulate his brain. In return, I got to bond with him again after so many years away.

Most of the time, my mother's and my arrangement is a wonderful exchange: we give each other things we need, and we each get something back. Sometimes, however, I wonder whether my mother and I push too hard to keep my father in our world.

One thing my mother has wanted to do more of, but which has been difficult to accomplish since my father's disease has gotten worse, is to attend cultural activities—musical performances, concerts and plays, museum exhibitions. She hasn't been going to events like this very much over the past few years, partly because, as most caregivers discover, it's just so difficult to do almost anything with an Alzheimer's patient. But now that I'm here, why couldn't she go out on her own? I wondered, Why doesn't she participate in community gatherings, see friends, go to dinner parties, attend concerts, even if it means going without my father? Why does the world of the caregiver—and the world of the Alzheimer's patient—become so small?

I have been trying to answer this question for some time, and especially since I have come home to help out. I often joke with my mother that she has Stockholm Syndrome (named for those hostages in Sweden in 1973 who, when they were given the chance at freedom, chose to stay with their captors). But the captor isn't my father. It's Alzheimer's.

Now that I've been home for a while, I'm afraid I might be getting Stockholm Syndrome, too. It isn't rational. There is no basis for this. But at times I am afraid to leave because I think he might die while I'm gone. At other times I don't want to leave because I think that perhaps the father he used to be will come back, or he'll remember something important, a moment from my childhood— a glimmer of him will appear once again, and I'll miss it. I won't be there to see the old Dad in his eyes.

Maybe that's why my mother can't leave, either. She's afraid she'll miss being with her husband again, even if he comes back for only a few seconds while she's gone.

Sometimes I say to her, "You can't leave. Why can't you leave?"

"I can't explain it," she replies.

So I will try. I think that, as a caregiver, you get caught in a trap. Even if a friend is willing to help, even if day care is available to take care of your loved one for a few hours, some internal feeling makes you unable to go out and have a good time. My theory is that it's partly guilt: you feel bad when you go off to do something fun while your loved one is left behind to suffer. But also it's that when the person with Alzheimer's *does* finally go somewhere, leaves the house for day care or is taken on an outing by a friend, you just want to be alone in the house by yourself and learn how to breathe again without the pain. You just want to pour a cup of tea and stare into space and feel the quiet without sensing the suffering that seeps from the chair where the person with Alzheimer's sits and hangs his head.

The sadness is palpable in my parents' house. My father's anguish spreads from my parents' bedroom to the hallway to the kitchen, where, in the morning, he scrapes his spoon repeatedly against the cereal bowl. I can feel it when I wake up. It throbs, this pervasive pain. I have been experiencing it for more than two years now, but my mother has lived with it for more than a dozen.

There's another reason we can't seem to attend as many activities as we'd like, and why, when we do go out, we end up taking my father with us. I think it's that my mother loves my father so much that she has decided to endure the difficulty and the awkwardness and the potential for embarrassment, just to give him a moment or two of happiness. I've resigned myself to the fact that when we finally do get out the door to do something interesting or entertaining, we will probably go together, the three of us.

Going to the Detroit Institute of Arts has been at the top of a list of activities my mother has wanted to do. Because my mother and father are members, we were invited to preview a very special exhibit called Camille Claudel and Auguste Rodin: Fateful Encounter. We signed up for it, scheduled it, and decided to go for it despite the potential for problems.

There was to be a luncheon first, followed by a lecture, followed by a tour of the show about the two sculptors, which included more than a hundred of their combined works. We knew this was risky for Dad. It would probably not have been his favorite thing to do even before he had Alzheimer's, and he doesn't like to stand up for long periods of time. Nevertheless, we decided to try it, and once again, we did it as a threesome because, rather than go off to the luncheon and art show by herself, Mom wanted to share the day with Dad, and with me.

The luncheon went fine, though Dad asked lots of questions about why we had come to this place, what we were doing—the usual. He looked so handsome in his sports coat and dress pants, but he introduced himself to the people at our table several times, each time as if it were the first. I am getting used to seeing strangers' faces register: Hmm. There's something wrong here. I watched my mother's face, and when the people at the table realized that my dad is impaired, I saw something so very sad in her eyes. At first, she seemed indignant. Then I saw a moment of resignation. I realize she withdraws from him in those moments, and though she hasn't told me this, I suspect she has an internal dialogue that goes something like this: This is not the man I married. This is not the Woody I know. There is a kind of anguish that she tries to hide, a sense that his Alzheimer's is something she cannot cover for anymore.

Then, of course, after the people at the table have realized that my father will not be contributing normal conversation, the knots in my mother's and my stomachs begin to form as we move, with dread, toward the meal. Will the waitress ask him a question he can't answer, such as what kind of salad dressing he wants? Will we be able to step in to help in time, before he becomes embarrassed?

We did a good job of fending off these moments. We got through the soup and salad course just fine. But then, the biggest worry: utensils. You don't want to be cutting a person's food for them, whether you're in a diner or at a fancy members' luncheon at a museum. And we didn't want to embarrass Dad like that. But then, there he was, trying to cut his meat with a spoon. Mom stepped in to the situation discreetly. We made it through the meal without a big crisis.

We survived dessert and coffee with no major snafus and said good-bye to the folks with us at the table. Now, the next hurdle to cross—he needed to go to the restroom. I did the usual, guiding him to the correct bathroom door and waiting outside. He made it out of the bathroom and didn't wander away down the hallway or get lost.

Then we headed to a large auditorium to hear the lecture. My father understood that he should be quiet. He didn't whistle or talk loudly during the speech. He was doing his usual "reading of the room," in which he looks around at what others are doing and follows their lead. It's another example of how sensitive he has become since he got this disease.

We were able to learn how the two women in Rodin's life influenced his art. Dad crossed his legs, seemed to be listening to the speaker intently, and applauded at the proper times. Then we attended the exhibit. In the first gallery, as everyone else began to examine the sculptures and drawings, Dad basically just stood in the middle of the room, in a new leaning-forward way (he has started to shuffle and often stands in an awkward Alzheimer's-induced pose). It was clear he was not exactly sure where to look. It was quite clear to me that these sculptures didn't impress him. I could also see that his knees and his back were hurting. Meanwhile, everyone in the room except us was listening to a guided tour of the exhibit on headphones. It was very quiet. My mother and I were reading a detailed description of the process Rodin went through to sculpt one of his most famous works, *The Gates of Hell.* We turned around, and there was Dad, heading toward the platform on which the piece itself was being exhibited. He had a satisfied look on his face, as if he had just found out some secret that no one else knew, as he pointed toward the platform and said, "I'm just going to sit down and rest on this!" We rushed over, whispering urgently, "No, *no*, you can't sit down there!"

The people wearing their museum headsets looked alarmed at the flurry of activity. It was a close call. We found a proper museum bench where my father could sit, and my mother and I continued to look at the sculptures and drawings. Dad, suddenly rejuvenated, walked with us and took an interest in one of the sculptures. We moved into a new room and were looking at several busts sculpted by Claudel. It was then that Dad shuffled up to me and asked loudly, so that even the people with the headsets could hear, "Why are we here?"

At that moment, I thought, He has a point. Why *are* we here? Some of the people around us chuckled. Maybe they were wondering the same thing.

We moved into the next room of exhibits. Dad said he wanted to sit down, but this time, there was no museum bench to sit on. We tried to interest him in some of the drawings. Mom and I became involved with a description of a house in the country where Claudel and Rodin had lived happily and created many pieces of art before their affair ended. In my peripheral vision, I could see Dad sort of rocking back and forth on the balls of his feet. Dad moved toward me and said he wanted to rest his legs for a minute. He said he would "just lean on this." He started to lean over toward something, and I realized, suddenly, that it was not a pole, or a post, or a hat rack, or a railing. It was one of the first bronze castings of Rodin's famous sculpture of *The Thinker!*

Many potential calamities raced through my mind. "No, no, Dad, don't lean on that!" I shouted. I hated the tone of my voice. I sounded like a mother chastising a child. The museum guards, at this point, were quite nervous. We stopped Dad before his hand touched the clenched fist of *The Thinker's* left arm.

Somehow, we made it out of the museum with no breakage and no arrests. Dad didn't try to lean on any pieces of art in the last two galleries. When we got back to the car, I wondered whether it was worth it for Dad or for us to do this kind of outing anymore. Maybe we'd been taking him to too many places. Maybe we'd been putting him in situations we shouldn't have been putting him in. Maybe it was time to stop trying to do things like this anymore.

Perhaps all family caregivers of Alzheimer's patients lie to themselves. Perhaps they tell themselves things will get better in order to survive. Maybe I deluded myself when I came home and thought, somehow, that I would be able to fix him. Instead, despite everything you do to try to help the situation, it's like watching someone slowly drowning underwater or sinking in quicksand.

There are times I have wondered whether it is worth it—for me and for my parents. Am I only prolonging the pain? Is my mother's life, and is my life, spiraling downward, with no positive outcome and no change in the quality of my mother's and father's lives?

Almost every time I feel depressed and lost and worried that I may have messed up my life forever and not even helped my father or my mother by coming home, my father seems to intuit my hopelessness and comes through with some sort of gem to keep me going, a lesson that helps me look at the bigger picture. For instance, the other day, I took him driving around to look at the fall colors. Brilliant yellows and reds blazed around the shore of the lake near our cottage. We listened to CDs and sang along to recordings of his a cappella singing group, the Grunyons. I brought up the fact that he was going to be turning eighty years old, and I said, "Dad, why don't we have a party to celebrate?" He answered, "Am I wise enough for all of that?" I said, "Yes, Dad! I think you would enjoy it!"

It was strange how he framed his words. It was an acknowledgment of his disease. "Am I wise enough?" was his way of saying, "Am I smart enough? Will I understand it enough?" It's as if he can stand outside of himself, judging what's going on, despite having had Alzheimer's for so many years.

Then he said, "I don't think I'm very good." I told him how well he was doing, particularly for someone who has had Alzheimer's for more than a decade. I told him we could get his singing group and all his old friends to come to the party. He said, "That would be fun," and then he added, "It's true. I have lovely people around me."

It was one of those blowy midwestern autumn days when the sky turns gray, there's rain, then the sun punches through the clouds and there's a burst of blue and sunshine. Sheets of rain sparkled as the sun hit them. I explained to Dad about how the sun and the rain together meant a rainbow might appear. We started looking for a rainbow together, and suddenly there it was above us—a double rainbow stretching in an almost Technicolor arc across the sky. I had never seen a rainbow so brilliant and so huge. I asked Dad if he wanted to try to follow the rainbow to its very end, and he said, "Yes!" We drove to the edge of the lake, where it seemed that the rainbow plunged directly into the clear navy-blue water. I said, "Is it okay if we just drive around like this, Dad?" and he said, "Yes. Let's take our time. Easy. Don't do any rushing." It was as if he got it—the significance of the rainbow, the awe of it, that it was something magic you must stop for and appreciate. It was the first time he had "tuned in" in a long time.

Then he said, "I can't tell you what it means to me that you are here."

Moments. They're all we have. Maybe they're all any of us ever have.

Chapter Four

Alzheimer's Chicken

TODAY I WENT INTO MY CLOSET TO find my favorite pair of black pants. After searching for some time, I finally recognized them. They were hanging inside out, the waistband snarled around the top of the hanger, the crease of the pants in the center of the legs rather than at the sides, the pant legs twisted and hanging upside down. I took them off the hanger and put them on, even though the crease was in the wrong place. Then I searched for the matching black top. It was wrapped around the bottom rung of the hanger. The sleeve was inserted in the loop of the wire where it hangs off the rack. I untangled it and tried to smooth the wrinkles out.

Many of my clothes are hanging this way in my closet. This is because my father helps me hang up my clothes. It's something I have chosen for us to do together because if he doesn't do it properly, the consequences are not so great. Nothing can spill. Nothing can break. Nothing can catch on fire. I have decided that rather than telling him he's doing it wrong, I'll just let him hang my pants upside down. And I'll wear slightly wrinkled clothes. (Though I have been learning about domestic chores since I came home, I simply cannot bring myself to iron except in dire emergency-type situations.)

Sometimes I go into the closet to rehang the clothes after Dad goes downstairs. But it seems rude to undo his work, so I leave a lot of the clothes the way he has chosen to hang them. The truth is I kind of like looking in my closet and seeing my father's handiwork there. It's amusing. It's creative. It also reflects how things are upside down in his brain. It also announces to me and to others that things are not normal in this house. We are not going to pretend, anymore, that everything's okay. Our house is not going to look like most people's houses. We are not going to follow the rules of normal living for a very good reason—to incorporate a person living with Alzheimer's into our lives. It's a worthwhile exchange—a messy closet and some wrinkled clothes for a father who feels useful and loved and part of our lives. It seems to me that doing this chore helps his self-esteem, and if nothing else, it's something we can do together. The other day, I thought, My closet represents how life gets turned around when living with someone who has Alzheimer's.

Dad and I also make beds together. It's something else that has soft edges and only minimal consequences in the event he doesn't do it the way most people do. Sometimes the blanket is placed on the bed upside down and the sheet is put on sideways, but compared to so many other things, these are such minor setbacks in the scheme of life. Frankly, he often makes the bed much better than I do. Until recently, he refused to walk out of a room where the bed was unmade. It seems to bother him terribly. He says one of two things: "Don't we have to put this off?" or, "Shouldn't we turn this off?" as he points to an unmade bed. Then he begins the task of "turning off" the bed.

Dad took on the chore of making the beds as soon as he retired, and even now that Alzheimer's has ravaged his brain, he continues to make beds with zeal and even, perhaps, a sense of pride. He spends a lot of time smoothing the surface of the blanket or the cover. He used to make sure all the edges were straight, but he does this less as his Alzheimer's progresses. He and my mother made their bed together every morning before I came home to help out, and he continues to do so, often completely by himself. He still makes the bed he shares with my mother on his own, and sometimes with no prompting from anyone. My mother tuned in, early on, to what chores would be good for my father to do as his Alzheimer's began to take hold, and she purposefully encouraged him to do the things he did well.

I have carried on the habit of Dad and I making various beds together in our house near Detroit and at our cottage in northern Michigan. My mother even taught him, before Alzheimer's, to arrange a collection of designer pillows on top of their bed properly. So even though there are times he can't find his way to the bedroom, somehow the beds are usually beautifully made and the pillows are almost always placed the way my mother taught him to do it. My theory is that making the bed and arranging the pillows is one place where he remembers how to have order in his life, even though his own brain is in such chaos.

The same sense of order applies to food. After he finishes eating his meal, he has taken to arranging the leftovers on his plate in a symmetrical way, and he will often put his silverware in perfect diagonals across the edges of the plate. Recently, when he helps to clean up the kitchen, he makes what I call "setups" with leftover food, napkins, and silverware. He once placed two lemon slices at the top of the plate and a single grape at the bottom in the shape of a face with two eyes and a mouth. He makes colorful arrangements with leftovers such as beets and broccoli florets. My father has become The Alzheimer's Designer.

When he helps us clean the kitchen, we often can't locate the cleaning supplies for some time. We find sponges and rags arranged like soft sculptures in the corners of the kitchen, sometimes wedged next to the coffee pot or between the stove and the counter, standing up. Once I discovered a pink sponge wedged in a vertical position between the toaster and the wall. The other day I couldn't find a Windex bottle for a very long time. Eventually, I discovered it hanging in the center of the headboard of my bed, like a kind of figurehead.

My mother says it was a long and slow progression until she finally understood that my father could no longer help her do certain chores. She says she doesn't really remember how and when it happened, but she started having to show him where the dishes went and how to set the table. Certain tasks he had done his whole life simply fell away. She says she would tell him to go out to get the mail and after about ten minutes, he would come back inside the house and say, "Where's the mail?" He no longer knew what a mailbox was, or where it was. "It was shocking," she said. She would ask him to do a fairly simple chore, such as taking an object from one room to the next, and he couldn't retain the instructions.

These days, as my father's brain atrophies more, bizarre events occur. Recently, my mother discovered him sitting on the edge of their bed, trying to pull his T-shirt over his legs and wondering why it didn't fit better. He had put his legs through the armholes and pulled the bottom of the shirt up over his thighs and waist. Some days, he wears two sweaters. My mother usually lays his clothes out for him, but there are times he beats her to it or adds his own creative fashion choices.

As his Alzheimer's progresses, there are even more unusual twists and turns in what my father does. One day, I was in a hurry and looking all over the house for my purse. It was time for an appointment, and I was doing that frantic "Where the hell is it? What did I do with it?" routine. It was time to go. I was looking under couches, under beds, searching nooks and crannies. Was it hung on a hook on the back of my closet door? In the entranceway where I sometimes put my keys? Nothing. Nowhere.

This was one of my favorite purses. I had bought it long ago on vacation in Miami from a fancy store in South Beach. It was handmade with red flowers and sparkles embroidered into it. It actually looks more like a piece of artwork than a purse.

Now, it had vanished, as if into thin air. It was summer, and there were ten of us staying at the cottage. The entire household wound up helping me search for my purse. Everyone seemed to assume I had left it somewhere accidentally, but I *knew* I had brought it home and put it in my bedroom and it had just disappeared. I was very, very frustrated. I looked at Dad and thought, He must have something to do with it. (He must be getting used to seeing that accusing look when we can't find something. A person living with Alzheimer's is a convenient scapegoat when things go wrong.) We looked through my father's things, even, wondering if he might have mistakenly snatched it. Again, nothing. Finally, I went off to the appointment without my purse and, thus, without my driver's license. I worried that I might get into an accident and I wouldn't have my license with me.

When I got back home from the appointment, I looked around the house again. I was very frustrated and searched the house until late at night. When it was time to go to sleep, I pulled back the bedspread. My father had helped me make my bed that morning. There, arranged beautifully between the pillows, was my fancy, sparkly purse. It actually looked very attractive. He must have thought it was a decorative pillow.

These are the things that happen when you live with someone who has Alzheimer's. Sometimes they are simply sweet reminders. Other times they can cause a major glitch in your day, or more.

Some things Dad does that cause difficulty for others could be prevented by constant monitoring, but we often don't have the time to watch him while he does chores. Also, it feels very condescending to do so. My mother and I want to be able to leave him alone so he can do things on his own and feel more independent. Yet when we do that, we know that problems might arise.

I recall one time Dad helped me to bring groceries into the house from the car. I wanted to believe he could do this on his own, so I carried armfuls of groceries into the house while he grabbed the next load from the back of the car. It seemed simple enough. All he had to do was grab the bags and bring them inside.

He brought the last bag of groceries in. He even slammed the trunk of the car to close it properly. Everything seemed to be going along just fine. We put away food together, making sure the perishables went in the right places. I have to tell him where each thing goes, no matter how many times we have done this together. No matter how many times my mother and father did this together for more than fifty years, it is all brand new now. We have learned how to do this together, the three of us, since I came home. This is our routine: starting over again with each object, saying where the refrigerator is, where the cupboard is, each time he holds something up and doesn't know where it goes.

"Milk goes in the refrigerator."

"Refrigerator?"

"It's that big white door on the right."

"This door?"

"No, not the left door. That's the freezer."

"What is this?"

"That's a bottle of juice, Dad. You are holding it upside down. You hold it like this, with the narrow part facing up, so it won't spill."

"Where does this go?"

"That's butter. It goes in that little box with the door. Here's how you open the door."

"Where does this go?"

"That's broccoli. The vegetables go in this bin."

Often I think, How can't he know that, after so many years of using that same refrigerator and that same cupboard and that same bread box and that same pantry in this same house?

Almost every chore done with an Alzheimer's patient takes twice as long, but finally, we were done. All the groceries were put away, and even the plastic bags and grocery bags were folded and placed in the proper cupboard.

Two days later, we were driving in the car. Something smelled funny. I stopped to check the back of the car and found various pieces of fruit, yogurt, and a half gallon of milk rolling around. Then I realized that he hadn't seen the items fall out of the grocery bag the other day. I made a mental note that I have to be with him for the last load of groceries he takes out of the car. I realized he no longer has the capacity to notice that objects have fallen out of the grocery bags. It is not in his vision anymore. It is not part of his reasoning. It is not a concern of his anymore. Like many tasks, it is something else that has simply "fallen away."

But then, after we got home that day, I realized that something else was amiss, more than the fact that produce and yogurt and milk had been left to rot in the back of the car. The emergency kit and the flashlight and the road map that I keep in the back of the car were missing. A lightbulb went on. Hmmm. He had taken those things inside instead of the groceries he was supposed to bring in the house! So now, where could those things be? That was another chore for the day—find the things my father brought inside that were supposed to stay in the car.

Doing damage control is exhausting. I don't know how anyone can do it alone. Yet my mother has been doing alone a version of what I just described for more than ten years. No wonder she seems so stressed and tired. Each day, what my father can and cannot do changes. Sometimes in just a matter of hours, a task he once could do disappears from his repertoire. But I know that my mother believes that including my father in tasks and chores is worth the difficulty if it makes him feel included and loved and keeps him at home with us.

Recently we asked Dad to take the kitchen trash outside. We pointed to the proper receptacle. We saw him take the white plastic trash can out the door and dump the stuff in the large receptacle for pickup day. Then my mother and I went back to whatever we were doing. The next day, the white plastic trash can was nowhere to be found. How could a rather large white trash can disappear? A search through the house turned up nothing. Finally, my mother went into the guest bathroom and opened the shower door. There it was on the floor of the shower, sitting on top of the drain. We couldn't figure out why he would choose this spot. What did the trash can remind him of? Perhaps he couldn't find us when he didn't know where to put it, and he wanted to hide it somewhere so we wouldn't realize he didn't know where it belonged.

My mother and I pick and choose the chores my father can do on a day-to-day basis. The truth is, though, when we are exhausted and there are many appointments to keep and we are in a terrible mood and he is having a bad day, too, we don't involve him at all. When the patience needed to involve him just isn't there, and if we are upset or angry, he can sometimes sense our unhappiness and impatience, and it upsets him, too. Those are the days we decide it's okay to have him sit and watch TV ("the radio") (preferably CNN or an old movie) while we do all the chores by ourselves. Sometimes, we just have to let him check out, and sometimes we need to check out, too, because sometimes, being a caregiver is exhausting. Being someone who has Alzheimer's must sometimes be exhausting, too.

There is one household chore my dad does without fail. It is something he can always do, no matter how badly both our days are going. And he does it with a surprising amount of determination and sense of responsibility (whistling all the while) as he embraces the familiarity of the task. The memory of what it is and what he must do has never gone away as long as I have been home with him. He folds laundry beautifully. This is something my father has in common with lots of people who have Alzheimer's. Whenever I visit a facility that specializes in Alzheimer's patients, there is a basket filled with laundry that needs to be folded (or sometimes just a pile of socks) in the corner.

Harvard Health Publications Web site, in a description of long-term residential care options for Alzheimer's patients, describes the following:

> Many of these facilities strive to keep the Alzheimer's patient active and offer a wide array of activities that involve all residents at different levels of ability. The activities should be set up so they provide some meaning and enjoyment to the individual without too much stimulation or pressure to learn. Some examples include participating in arts and crafts projects, going through family photographs, engaging in appropriate exercise, singing, dancing, listening to music, or doing chores, such as folding laundry, which may be enjoyable for some but meaningless to others.

The feel of warm, clean clothing coming out of the dryer is soothing for all of us, but maybe even more so for an Alzheimer's patient. It's something almost every patient seems to embrace. If you watch people in a memory care facility folding in a group, you will see an amazing similarity—the way many of them hold up the clothes for some time, examining each piece to determine what it is, the slow recognition of a sleeve, a pant leg, a towel, or an undergarment. You will see the intense studiousness involved in the chore of trying to match socks. Perhaps most important to this task is the fact that they can take as long as they need to do it. It is not a time-sensitive activity. You can leave them alone to fold laundry and almost nothing bad can happen (except for the possibility that some of the clothes could be misplaced. You might find a sock or shirt tucked under a pillow on a nearby sofa. Or the pile of folded clothes might wind up in an unusual place.) You could put a video camera on Alzheimer's patients in almost any care facility, and you would see them moving together in rhythm as they fold, like a beautiful and tragic dance.

Of course, some of the laundry will be folded inside out, and the socks put together in pairs won't always match. But it doesn't matter. You can always put your shirt right side out when it's time to put it on. And the two socks that go together will eventually find each other. Like so many things I have learned since I came home, the greater outcome of doing the chore with the Alzheimer's patient outweighs whether the chore is done properly. It's one of the many lessons I have learned about helping a person with Alzheimer's stay in this world.

When Dad's Alzheimer's started getting worse, one of the most exasperating things for my mother was to constantly repeat instructions as they tried to do various chores together. Explaining over and over again how to do a simple daily chore, mixed with my father's inability to do so many things, was extremely exhausting for her. She was running out of things he could still do in their home, but one thing he seemed to never forget how to do was vacuum. He seemed to have a knack for it. He couldn't remember how to turn the machine on or off, so she had to do that part of the task for him, but once the sound of the vacuum kicked in and she placed the contraption in his hand, he suddenly remembered what it was and began expertly running the vacuum nozzle along carpets, as well as the brick and hardwood floors. Sometimes, even when the house was clean, Mom would have him vacuum something so he'd feel useful and she'd get a break from having to explain things to him, or from having him simply sit in front of the TV while she felt guilty about leaving him there.

The vacuuming started to become a family joke. My older sister, Alison, said it seemed that whenever she called home, she could hear the hum and whine of the vacuum in the background. She even questioned Mom about making Dad vacuum so much. "What the hell is with the vacuuming?" I heard her say. I think she wondered whether Dad actually enjoyed it and even implied that Mom was treating him like hired help. My mother became indignant and took offense. Finally, she said loudly to all of us one day, "I have him vacuum a lot because it's one of the few things he can still do!"

Now, I understand more clearly why she did this and why the sound of the vacuum was so pervasive. It is one of the few chores he can accomplish without constant supervision. At first, when I came home, I watched Dad vacuum quite thoroughly, even behind pieces of furniture and in the corners. He still checked to make sure the contraption was working properly by placing his big hand against the nozzle to feel the suction. Even though he vacuumed the house so well, he sometimes would begin the chore with the vacuum nozzle upside down. These days, he sometimes misses corners. Sometimes big swatches of carpet still have quite a few crumbs left when he thinks he's done. And yes, at times dust and dirt are left behind. When that happens, we go back and run the vacuum over those spots again. It doesn't take much time—like the clothes hanging in the closet, the sponges left in strange places, and the laundry folded inside out.

What is most important? Him. Not whether the house is clean. Not whether the clothes in the closet are hanging up properly. Him, and whether he is doing things with us and feeling useful, instead of just sitting in front of the TV. This is simply what you do with someone who has Alzheimer's who can still participate in life. I remember thinking that this must be what many parents experience with their young children. Except in this instance, the learning curve was mine.

Every day, when you help take care of someone who has Alzheimer's, you go through a litany of conversations in your head. You go from the way life used to be before Alzheimer's to the way life is after Alzheimer's. You change your standards, and you change your sense of time. You say to yourself, What is important? So what if it takes a long time to accomplish a task?

The following recipe illustrates a theory about taking care of someone who has Alzheimer's. It's a recipe for a kind of chicken my father and I make together, but it's also a recipe for including a person living with Alzheimer's in your life.

Alzheimer's Chicken

whole chicken, about 4 pounds
1 green apple, washed and cored
3 stalks of celery, rinsed
1 yellow or white onion, skin removed
several sprigs of fresh rosemary, sage, and thyme,
    rinsed
½ cup red wine
3 tablespoons olive oil

Preheat oven to 350°. Rinse a 4-pound roasting chicken, removing and discarding the giblets from the cavity.

Place the green apple, celery, onion, and herbs on a large chopping board. Hand a not-so-sharp knife to the Alzheimer's patient, depending of course on how far the disease has progressed. It may not be wise to do this for Alzheimer's patients who've been living with the disease for more than ten years, but my father can still safely use a knife if I stand next to him and make sure he isn't holding it upside down.

Let the patient chop up the fruit, vegetables, and herbs however the hell he or she wants to, without hovering and explaining how to do it! Don't say: "No! Do it like this!" Remember: It doesn't matter what the chunks look like or how big or small they are. The process can be liberating not only for the patient but also for you.

Open up the cavity of the chicken and have the Alzheimer's patient help you stuff the vegetables, fruit, and herbs into the bird with a big wooden spoon. Put the chicken in a 9 × 13 inch baking dish or pan. Pour the red wine, olive oil, and a little water over the stuffed chicken. Cook it in the oven at 350° for at least two hours, until the temperature of the thigh reaches 180°. Have the Alzheimer's patient help you baste the bird often. Let it sit a bit after you've taken it out of the oven; then slice and serve.

The aroma of this chicken will fill the house, and it will remind you that an Alzheimer's patient can, in some way, still be part of making dinner when you have the time. (Also, if you've had a difficult day of caregiving or other work, warm, aromatic food cooking in the oven can be comforting.) You can usually find a smile together somewhere between chopping the celery and stuffing the bird. Singing together in the kitchen while you do chores like this is always a good thing to do. Ultimately, it feels good to do something like this with someone you love, whether or not they have Alzheimer's. Doing a chore like this together translates to: This person is still a functioning part of this family. This person can still be a useful part of society.

I promise you the chicken will taste delicious, no matter how badly and misshapen the vegetables and fruit are cut. Who cares what the stuffing looks like? When you take the juicy, golden brown chicken out of the oven, remind the Alzheimer's patient how much he or she helped to make the dinner. It will make the chicken taste even better.

Remember this when you clean, when you cook, when you make

beds, when you fold laundry, when you wash the car: It doesn't have to be perfect. It's more important that the Alzheimer's patient helped you do it. If you change your standards and if you are not a perfectionist about things, then the Alzheimer's patient can come along with you and help you do so many things. I believe in the case of my father that it helps his self-esteem to involve him in these things.

So, Rule Number One: Change your standards. This will allow you to share activities in a meaningful way with the person you love who has Alzheimer's.

Chores, tasks, and activities will go so much more quickly in the future when my father is no longer here. The rug he once vacuumed will be cleaner, too. I am not sure any of us will be able to make a bed as well as he does. The pieces of granny smith apples and celery and onions will be uniform and much smaller. I know I will miss him most when I am chopping the vegetables and fruit for the chicken. I doubt it will taste as good without him. When my mother takes the laundry out of the dryer, it will be so strange not to have my father there to fold the clothes, even though he sometimes folds the clothes inside out . . . and the socks don't match . . . and the clothes wind up under pillows.

When he is gone, everything will be in its proper place. Except for my father.

Some of the routines my father has taken on of late have become obsessions. He must turn out the lights in almost all the rooms he exits. (Once he tried to do so in a museum! As you can imagine, the security guards didn't like it much.) Some evenings, my mother or I will be in the family room or living room in the middle of an activity and he won't realize this and will turn out the light. "Dad . . . don't!" comes the cry in the darkness. He always apologizes. Then, moments later, he will do it again, because he has already forgotten we are there and we told him not to. It's difficult when we are in the middle of doing something such as reading.

My mother says he must think light is evil. Or maybe it's a belief left over from the 1930s Depression era, that lights sap energy and dollars. Whatever the reason, he is obsessed with turning out the lights. These days he just doesn't want to see a light left on anywhere in the house, or in other people's houses, or even in stores. So, we end up sitting in the dark sometimes. We bump into things in rooms that previously used to have lamps or small lights left on.

The other day I was reading in a room at night, and Dad didn't see me. He walked in and turned out the light. I just sat there in the dark for a while because I didn't have the heart to tell him to turn the light back on (it was, once again, more evidence that he had done something wrong). I waited for him to move to another room and then turned the light back on.

I don't mind sitting in the dark right now, because I know that someday my mother and I will be turning the lights on and off for ourselves without him. A lot of us who love someone with Alzheimer's are sitting in the dark, waiting for the next light to go out. I hope I am with my father when he turns out the last light.

Chapter Five

Swoonboy

Canada geese are monogamous. Pairs form during the winter, during migration or on their wintering grounds, for the next breeding season. Mated pairs may stay together for more than one year, sometimes staying together for life.
   —*from the Animal Diversity Web, an online database of animal natural history, distribution, classification, and conservation biology at the University of Michigan*

A FRIEND OF MINE WHO LIVES IN northern Michigan says his father, who had taught tracking and hunting and served as a guide in the Upper Peninsula, quit hunting one day and for a very specific reason. It was because of an incident that occurred when he and his friends were shooting geese near Pt. Pelee in Windsor, Canada. He saw a flock going over in V formation. He zeroed in on the last large goose in the flock. The gun went off. It wasn't a clean hit. He saw the wounded bird begin to lose altitude. The bird fell slowly, trying to save itself. He waited to see if the bird would plummet and if the trained dogs with him would retrieve it. Then he saw something he had never seen before. A bird from the front of the V suddenly pulled out of formation and soared beneath the wounded bird as it fell, cradling it on its wings as it helped to bring the wounded bird back up to the V. My friend's father said he was so stunned he simply put his gun down and watched. He presumed this was the bird's mate (Canada geese are known to mate for life). He watched as the healthy bird continued to carry the wounded one on its back until it began to be dragged down by the weight. He watched silently as the birds disappeared in the distance, with the healthy bird and the injured bird on its back wobbling below the flock. He thought, Now neither of them will make it to their southern destinations (he figured they were headed some 1,500 miles away). Most likely, the healthy bird went down with the injured mate, and all because he and his friends were out to smell the cold autumn air and traipse through the woods with their weapons and dogs and fire guns into the sky to prove who had the best aim.

He said his father stood in the woods for some time thinking about a partnership so strong you would jeopardize your own life to save another. After that, my friend's father went out into the woods with other hunters. He often went with his son, who shot birds and deer in the fall. But he never raised his gun to shoot an animal again.

Since my father got Alzheimer's, my mother has been carrying him on her wings. But what if, like the bird that got out of formation to carry the injured bird on its back, she goes down with him, too?

The other day, my father and I were sitting by the fire at the cottage on the lake. My mother was in the kitchen. Dad pointed to my mother and said to me, "How did I meet her?" So now, as I often tell my father these days, I will tell *you* how they met.

Swoonboy. That's the coveted title my father, Woody Geist, won in a popularity contest when he was a freshman at Wayne State University in Detroit. He was six-foot-two, had recently gotten a trendy crew cut, and sometimes wore a white suit and bow tie to parties. He had earned a spot on the college basketball and tennis teams after lettering in several sports in high school. He was known to burst into song often and had learned all the latest dance steps. The women who voted for him in the Swoonboy competition said he sang and danced like Frank Sinatra.

World War II was nearing an end, but my father knew he could be drafted at any time. The air was electric with possibility and drama. Everyone knew that if you served overseas, you might not come back alive, and that if you *did* make it back home, your life might be changed forever.

Before he got Alzheimer's, when my father used to speak about this period of his life, his eyes would light up. It was clear that it was an exhilarating time for him, a time when he tested his limits, discovered who he was and what he might become. Drafted before his sophomore year in college, Woody was trained as a jungle fighter. My mother, Rosemary, laughs when she talks about this, because the very idea of my father—a sweet and gentle soul with skinny legs—becoming a jungle fighter seemed absurd to her. I doubt he could commit an act of violence against anyone. The most violent he has ever become is when he cussed himself out on the golf course after missing a shot.

The war ended just in time. My father wound up serving in the medical corps in Germany, treating soldiers for venereal diseases they had contracted during the war and playing tennis across Europe for the U.S. Army team. It wasn't exactly the combat zone he had expected. When he came back home, he transferred from Wayne State to the University of Michigan on the G.I. Bill.

If not for the war, my father wouldn't have met my mother. It was early evening in the spring of 1948 at the University of Michigan. My mother was in a sorority. My father, who had just returned from Germany after serving in the war, was in a fraternity. My father came to the Kappa Kappa Gamma house to pick up my mother's roommate for a date. He was wearing a white tie and tails because he was about to perform in a concert with the University of Michigan Glee Club. My mother, who was about to go on a date with Dad's fraternity brother, was at the top of the stairs and my father was at the bottom. In this way, their eyes first met, my mother looking down on him, my father looking up at her. Neither of them has ever seemed to be able to articulate why this moment stands out in their minds. I have a hunch that, like other people I have talked with who fell in love at first sight, in that moment they could somehow see the future in each other. They could see their children in each other's eyes, the home they'd have someday, and they could somehow see—even in that split second of time—that they would take care of each other when they grew old. My mother said this to me about her relationship with my father: "It seemed inevitable. It wasn't really like I had a choice."

My father didn't start dating my mother right away. It took him two months to muster the courage to ask her out. That summer, my father found my mother's home number where her parents lived in Ferndale outside of Detroit, and one day, "out of the blue," my mother says, he simply called her up and asked her out. My mother immediately said yes. (It is January 6, 2007, and my father, as he listened to my mother tell the story of their meeting, just said, "Do you think you did the right thing?" and then he laughed!)

She was smart, talented, and beautiful and came from a socially and politically involved, liberal family. He was smart, talented, and handsome, and though his family was more conservative, he shared liberal views with my mother.

They both loved music. They both planned to be teachers. They both wanted a family. They both had quirky senses of humor. It is easy to list the things my mother and father had in common. However, lots of people have things in common and never marry. What is it that makes two people able to fast forward to the future and say yes? Since I did it once, and it didn't work out, I am afraid to trust my instincts, and I wonder often about the element in a relationship that makes two people able to take this leap of faith.

My mother says on their first date, when she was twenty and he was twenty-two, my father took her to a friend's cottage on Lake St. Clair. They spent the day motoring in a boat on the lake. At the end of the date, as he dropped her off at her parents' home, my father, in a move considered very forward for the time, kissed my mother goodnight on the lips! My mother says, back then, the rule was that you should kiss only on the third date. So when he took her on the second date, my mother mentioned that they had broken the rules. My father called her bluff. He said, "Well, then, we don't have to kiss." Then, my mother says, she wanted to kiss him even more than she had before.

When they first began to date in the summer of 1948, they could see each other only every seven days because of my father's job at Borden's Creamery in Detroit. He had one day off a week, and they decided to make the most of it. They had a routine. He would pick my mother up early in the morning on the day he had off. Sometimes they would spend the day driving in the country; other times they might go to a jazz concert to see musicians such as Benny Goodman and Glenn Miller. Sometimes they would sing duets together (they both have beautiful voices) as they drove to beaches and lakes. They listened to Frank Sinatra records on rickety turntables. The dates almost always ended with long make-out sessions in my father's car parked in my grandfather's driveway. My mother admits that sometimes she didn't even get home until 3 or 4 a.m.

My mother says that after their first date together, my father went home and told his mother, Josephine, and his grandmother, affectionately known as Mama Ruthie (who was living with them in the family home), that he had met the woman he would marry. Several dates later, he brought my mother to his parents' house. My mother says, "When I arrived, Mama Ruthie ran from the parlor and said, 'Is this the woman Woody says he's going to marry?'" Woody's mother, Josephine, looked at my mother, whose face had turned bright red, and said, "I'd better get some ice for your face." My mother says she couldn't remember being that embarrassed in her entire life.

Of course, as it turns out, my father was right.

After the first summer of dating one day a week, they both returned to U of M. My mother says she "tried" to date a couple of other people, but soon there was only one man in her life. Not only was my father a full-time student at U of M, but he also worked as an orderly at a hospital. He got off his shift at 9:30 at night and would then pick up my mother from her sorority house. They would go to U Drug, a well-known pharmacy and soda shop on South University on the campus in Ann Arbor. They had exactly forty-five minutes to carry on some semblance of a date. She says, "We would usually just drink coffee and talk. Back then sororities were very strict. We had to be back at the house by 10:30." She says there were many other couples who would gather en masse on the porch of the sorority house to make out until the 10:30 curfew. The house mother rang a bell. The couples parted. Then the house mother would lock the doors.

In the spring of 1949, my father had a ring made out of his glee club pin and gave it to my mother. After that, my father made a decision. He wrote a heartfelt letter to my mother saying he couldn't go on this way—being in love and not being able to be together. He said he thought, even though they were both still in college, that the two of them should get married. My mother says she agreed, even though she felt the right thing to do would be to wait until they both got their degrees. They decided to take the bus from Ann Arbor to her father's office in Detroit to discuss it. She says my father stood behind her with his arms around her shoulders and announced to my grandfather that they wanted to get married. She says her father was very wise, that he smiled and said, "I'll help you in whatever way I can." Then she said, "Of course, this was absolutely the right move on my father's part."

That weekend my father got a ring from his father's jeweler.

Some time later, they went to the Detroit Golf Club to have a family engagement party, but they decided to wait until the following year to get married.

My mother graduated with a bachelor's degree from the School of Architecture and Design in June. She explained: "I started teaching, and I lived at home and taught in Royal Oak. Woody was still going to school at U of M because of the delay in his college education caused by the war."

My mother said, "I had to marry a man who was absolutely upstanding and honest and all those things. Other women I knew found more dangerous men attractive, but I had lived with wonderful men with great values. I couldn't marry anyone who was duplicitous. I needed to marry someone who was honest and straightforward and loving and kind because I'd known that, in my family, all my life."

It was a beautiful but simple wedding at my grandfather's church. My grandfather performed the ceremony. The reception was in the church parlor.

My mother says that one thing was clear in their relationship—though the marriage may have looked traditional to some, they were intellectual equals. They planned to change together, grow together, learn together. They read books together, and they talked and argued about politics. They were involved with local charities and the church. They shared common interests (except for tennis and golf). They talked about all the classes they would attend together when they retired, all the traveling and reading they would do, and all the adventures they would share.

She never dreamed she would wind up fighting a daily battle all by herself, even though he's by her side. Now, because of Alzheimer's, even though my father is still alive, my mother is alone. She has taken on all the responsibilities of the daily chores of their lives. As I write this, in June 2007, there isn't much left of the man he once was.

He is not really her partner anymore, though if you saw them walking hand in hand in the grocery store, or at the movies, or at a concert, you would know that, like the Canada geese, they are mated for life.

What can it be like to remember everything while your partner remembers nothing?

What can life be like for someone like my father, who can't look forward to the future because he can't imagine it? What can life be like now, when he can't look back because his memory has disappeared?

Yet somehow my father knows he loves my mother. He says it all the time. No future. No past. In some way, perhaps it is the perfect love. It exists on its own; it isn't fueled by the past or future, by memories, by what has happened or what is to be. It's just now. Joan Didion writes in her book *The Year of Magical Thinking* that "Marriage is memory, marriage is time." My father has almost no memory left. He can't remember the time.

How does love exist without the memory of love? I know it does. My parents do still have a marriage. They do love each other, even though it is tainted by Alzheimer's. Perhaps their love exists in the same way people describe love at first sight—you just know.

Once in a while, I have had to wake up my mother and father for an appointment (though usually my mother wakes up before me or my father). When I have peeked in on them in the morning, before they begin to stir, when they are in a deep sleep, they are spooned into each other, holding each other the way they always have. It appears that their bodies do not forget, not yet anyway, more than ten years into this disease. And their hearts do not forget. "What the heart has once owned and had, it shall never lose." That's what Henry Ward Beecher, the liberal Congregationalist clergyman and social reformer, wrote in the mid-1800s. Perhaps the emotion of love resides in a place the Alzheimer's plaque can't reach.

I have often wondered: What if they knew, then, when they were nineteen and twenty-one years old, that at age sixty-six, my father would begin to show signs of Alzheimer's disease? Would my mother have signed up for this? When my father asked her to marry him, if she knew this horrible disease would invade their lives four decades later, would she have said yes? The answer, I believe, is yes. Because even now, as Alzheimer's destroys my father's brain and changes almost every aspect of my parents' lives, the good in their lives together seems to outweigh the bad.

My mother and father forged an extraordinary life together in so many ways, and perhaps because of the strength of what they have built together, my mother can continue to have a relationship with my father, even as Alzheimer's takes him away. Their strong love helps her carry him on her wings.

But research shows that the spouse of someone with Alzheimer's is in a very precarious position. Doctors are now recognizing that when someone is diagnosed with Alzheimer's, the caregiver may require just as much attention as the patient, or more. Dr. Diana R. Kerwin, an assistant professor of medicine in the Division of Geriatrics and Gerontology at the Medical College of Wisconsin, says, "What we're seeing is that Alzheimer's is not a typical disease model, precisely because the health and well-being of the caregiver is affected as well as the patient. I know when I assume care of the Alzheimer's patient, I am also caring for the caregiver."

Caregivers who accompany patients to the Froedtert Senior Health Program's Geriatric Evaluation Clinic, where Dr. Kerwin practices, are screened for "caregiver stress" and see a gerontology nurse and social worker, who answer their questions, provide information, and help create a plan for the care of the patient. Caregivers are given a kit with information about support groups and community services, including adult day care, home care agencies, assisted living, skilled nursing facilities, and respite care.

The Alzheimer's Association says that more than 80 percent of Alzheimer's caregivers report that they frequently experience high levels of stress, and nearly half say they suffer from depression. The National Family Caregiver Alliance terms caregiver depression "one of today's all-too-silent health crises." The alliance estimates that caregiving spouses between the ages of sixty-six and ninety-six who are experiencing mental or emotional strain have a 63 percent higher risk of dying than people the same age who are not caregivers.

"Alzheimer's causes progressive memory loss, and in the later stages patients can develop behavior problems," Dr. Kerwin says. "It's distressing for the caregiver to suddenly have to cope with their loved one's anger, hallucinations, paranoia, aggression or inappropriate conduct in public. It's upsetting when, as the disease progresses, the patient no longer recognizes the spouse or loved one."

Caregivers often experience feelings of guilt, believing they are not doing enough to help, Kerwin adds. Spouses and adult children feel grief and loss, not unlike what they would experience following a death in the family. Alzheimer's is a progressively worsening disease, but the rate of progression from mild to advanced can vary widely, from three to twenty years. As Alzheimer's progresses, the loss of brain function itself will cause death unless the patient has one or more other serious illnesses.

Research shows that the caregiver, in the form of a spouse or family member, can make a huge difference in the life of an Alzheimer's patient, and in the cost of health care, too. In a recent study reported in the journal *Neurology*, researchers found that people with Alzheimer's disease may stay out of nursing homes longer if their spouses receive individualized support and counseling. Some four hundred caregiver-spouses of patients with Alzheimer's disease were randomly chosen for a specialized, university-based support program—including six sessions of individual and family counseling followed by ongoing support groups and telephone access to counselors—or to usual care, which included optional access to support services. Patients with Alzheimer's disease whose spouses received specialized support stayed out of nursing homes an average of one and a half years longer than those in the other group.

The researchers found that caregivers' increased satisfaction with social support, acceptance of patients' problem behaviors, and reduced depression accounted for most of the reduction in nursing home placement. The authors estimated an average cost savings of $90,000 per patient—"a pretty dramatic impact," says Peter Reed of the Alzheimer's Association, as quoted in *USA Today*.

There are no specific road maps for people with Alzheimer's disease and their caregivers, however, and every case is different. I talked with a man named Pat Hershey, whose wife was diagnosed with Alzheimer's at age fifty. I interviewed him in the fall of 2006, nine years after his wife's diagnosis. Early-onset Alzheimer's is a different road than my father's illness. Pat's wife, Kathy, at age fifty-nine, needs constant care. When I visited them in their home, a woman named Bonnie fed Kathy with a spoon in the kitchen. She seemed unable to move on her own and was sitting in a wheelchair. She could not speak. She only moaned a haunting sound that seemed to come from deep within her. She repeatedly tried to itch a spot on her neck like a swan preening on a lake, curled over. One eye seemed to be able to focus on objects; the other did not. I wanted to meet her one focused eye, but it was too heartbreaking to do so. I think she was trying to meet my eyes, too, straining and stretching to see me, as if to ask the question with her body: Who is this woman in my home? I couldn't help but wonder how much of her was still inside.

When Kathy turned forty-nine, Pat said, "I started noticing that her handwriting and spelling were changing. The school where she taught had a new principal. She started forgetting things. The student teacher would put something on her desk, and she'd forget it was there. Then a student would need medication, and she'd forget to give it to them. Basically, the principal just said, even though she had taught there for twenty-nine years, she couldn't do this anymore. They just wanted to get rid of her. Finally, our family doctor sent her to a neurologist.

"That was one of the most hurtful times for us," Pat explained. "We walked into the office for the exam. The doctor said, 'Do you know what floor you're on?' Well, she didn't do well. After we'd completed the first part of the exam, there was a knock on the door in the room where we were waiting. The doctor said, 'You have Alzheimer's, a form of dementia.'"

Kathy was devastated by the diagnosis. After that, Pat said there was a swift decline.

Pat and his wife decided they needed more opinions. "We went through the whole gamut of tests. We went to five different neurologists at the University of Cincinnati." Pat said it is clear that most people don't know how to handle this disease, especially when it is early-onset. In addition to the cold shoulder they got from the school where Kathy had worked most of her life, their social lives came to a screeching halt. "After six months, she no longer got calls from her teacher friends. I guess people just couldn't deal with it. Even her brother and sister didn't want to see it," he said.

One thing that helped was that their family doctor was a personal friend. "That's made a world of difference," Pat said. "When you go into the doctor's office and hear you're going into a new chapter in your life, it helped so much when he said, 'I want you to know I'm going to be going right along with you.'"

Kathy soon lost her ability to speak. Pat explained, "The only communication she has now is with food. She says 'Uh-huh' when I ask her if the food is good. She can hardly walk at all. Bonnie is with me at our summer home, and another person helps with hospice."

I asked Pat how he survives. The life the two of them once had together seems all but gone. Out of necessity and self-survival, Pat appears to function in the world during the day without her and comes home each evening to an invalid. He told me he knows this is not how she wanted things to end up when she learned she had early-onset Alzheimer's.

Pat said someone once asked him how he does it. His response was, "What's the alternative?" Kathy once told him not to let her get to the condition she's in now. "I want to be able to have some dignity," she told him. He told her he would do whatever she wanted him to do, at which point she said, "Pat, if I was a dog, you'd put me down."

"But I can't do it," he explained. "I can't. Sometimes I am afraid she will come back to haunt me after she's gone, because I am keeping her with me in this condition."

Alzheimer's disease affects patients and spouses in many different ways. I talked with Agnes Koch in January 2007. Agnes's husband, John, was diagnosed with Alzheimer's when he was seventy-four years old.

"The first signs were in 1992," she said. "We were getting ready to go out to dinner. He puts on a sport coat, shirt, and a tie and he was standing there for the longest time in the bedroom, and I said, 'What's wrong?' and he said, 'I forgot how to tie a tie.' I said, 'How could you forget how to tie a tie? You've been tying it for years!'

"Then shortly after that he had to deliver some special work to one of his best customers. He was still working full time. We were driving to this customer's plant, and he said, 'I forgot how to get there. I forgot what street it is.' I had been with him before to this place so I could tell him where to go. Then he was at work by himself one day and he said to me, 'There's somebody down there. I see them, they're by the machines down there.' I knew he was alone and I told him there was no one there, but he said, 'Yes they are, I can see them, they're working on the machines.'

"He was hallucinating. So those were the first signs. I didn't think that was too good, so I went to the library and I got the book *The 36-Hour Day*. I was not familiar with Alzheimer's at all. But I did some reading and talking with the kids. His oldest sister, Kate, had died of Alzheimer's. So we said we'd better look into that, and I read that book and I thought, Oh boy, you know there are so many symptoms there that he's exhibiting. That's how I caught on to the idea that he was afflicted with this.

"First we went to Dr. Trembly, an internist. He told us to go to a neurologist. The neurologist asked him the routine questions: 'What year is this? Who's the president?' He missed most of the answers.

"It shocked me. My husband was an intelligent man. He ran his own business for thirty-five years. He was in precision tool work. He went through a lot. He was in the military during World War II. He was always precise, on the ball, and knew many things about different fields. This really changed everything.

"The neurologist didn't help too much. There was no Aricept then. He had one drug, and when he was agitated I would give it to him, but it had an adverse effect. He got even more agitated and unreasonable. He'd hallucinate even more. He kept seeing things, people out the window. And then he got paranoid, especially about his wallet. He often thought people had taken money out of his wallet. This didn't happen all at once. It was gradual, of course.

"He kept working until May of 1993, when he sold the business. We owned the building and we owned the machinery and he just liquidated. We were fortunate to find people who would buy everything. He had no debts. And then he retired. He was home after that. I knew then we were on the road to Alzheimer's, but I didn't know where it was going to lead."

Agnes said she and her husband tried to maintain a social life, but, "when we did visit somebody, he just sat there and he didn't talk. At first, I was able to do things by myself. I belonged to two golf leagues. But he started resenting it when I left him alone in the house. And he did do strange things sometimes. Like, he would fall unexpectedly. Once we went out for a walk. We got up to the front door and he just keeled over and fell in the bushes. He did that many times. It took me about ten minutes to get him out of the bushes.

"About fours years after he was diagnosed, in '95 or '96, I was driving the car and one day he just said, 'Where's my wife? Why are you in this car?' I said, 'I *am* your wife.' He said, 'No, I want my *real* wife!' I said, 'I'm as real as you're going to get!'"

I asked Agnes if she went to an Alzheimer's support group. She said, "No, I didn't feel the need for it. I read the book. I knew what he was going through, and I knew I just had to take it. That's it. My father lived with us for twelve years after my mother died, and never, ever would I have put him in a nursing home or anything. It's my duty as his daughter and a member of the family to take care of him, and I wouldn't have it any other way. I feel the same way about my husband. I would never leave him. He was home. He died at home in 1999, seven years into the disease. In the end, that's what happened. He couldn't walk or get out of bed or anything.

"You know when I was really down in the dumps and sad was when he first no longer recognized me and treated me like a stranger. That was my hardest period. It took me quite a while to get adjusted to that. But after that, I realized he was going to die, and I felt I wanted to make things as pleasant for him as possible so that after he did die I would have a clear conscience, that I did the best I could for him to the end, and that's what I did. That's why I was able to resume my life, because I had done the best I could for him and everything was in order.

"What helped me a lot was my wonderful children. Boy, did

they come through for me." She choked up and was silent for a moment. "When I felt I was getting so tired, God took him. It just worked out that way. But there's no good ending."

My mother says her role as caregiver crept up on her. "It's like raising children," she said. "If you were dropped into it, you probably couldn't do it, but because Alzheimer's is a gradual thing, you adjust to each stage. It doesn't come on that suddenly. Things get a little harder as you go along, but you're still coping. You have to make a lot of adjustments. But sometimes there are sudden changes that shock you. All of a sudden you realize that he can't visualize anything. Then you realize he can't read anymore. You can't really be prepared for each stage. Each one is an adjustment, and there aren't any real plateaus. You keep thinking there are, and then everything changes again. He will hold up an umbrella and say, 'this wallet?' or he'll hold up the milk and say, 'this spoon?' He sees them, but he doesn't know what they are.

"He can't do much on his own anymore. At the beginning he could do everything. It started out with forgetfulness and not being sure where he was driving. Well, we're getting older, I thought. Even after the diagnosis, it wasn't really that noticeable for a number of years. It was so gradual.

"It's always been an option to move someplace else, and perhaps if one was going to do that one should do it early on," my mother said. "The whole moving and getting rid of everything becomes so difficult when one is impaired to that degree. Now, it would not be good for him to move. When we went to the first psychiatrist, Dr. Von Valtier, he told me the diagnosis was the worst thing that could happen to me. He said, 'After a long time, Woody will be happy, but you'll be very unhappy.'

"But that's not what happened because of Woody's unique situation. He's so aware and worried that he's a burden. He knows when I'm impatient. He's so sensitive. He's more empathetic since he got

Alzheimer's. He's always looking for clues: Is he all right? Is he doing the right thing? He's trying to pretend he can do things he can't, and then the more nervous he gets, the louder he whistles." (More than a decade into his disease, he whistles almost ten hours a day, almost the entire time he's awake.)

My mother chose to be the sole caregiver of my father as his Alzheimer's got worse. "I think it's what most wives would do," she said. "You very gradually take on the role of caregiver. You begin supervising everything—the house, all the paperwork, the investments. You just have to take on everything. As I said before, if you were just dropped into it, you would feel overwhelmed. It becomes more and more of a burden. I'm sure you reach a point where you feel you can't do it anymore. Some wives go on and keep doing it. Even when there's incontinence, they stick right with it to the end. I don't envision that for myself. I don't think I'm strong enough. Nor do I feel that I should."

My mother admits she has chosen to put her own life on hold to take care of my father. "As this person becomes the whole focus of your life, there's a direct relationship to how much of your life you lose. And when you get to a point where you feel that you're losing all your life. . . ." Her voice trailed off here. Then she explained: "Dad and I said when one or the other of us didn't know each other or who we are or where we are, then it's time to go to a residential facility. (Woody still refers to it as the 'looney bin.') The price is too great.

"I have the feeling most people would say it's like losing your parent; he's no longer there. But I don't feel that way so much with him. There's so much of Woody there. I know that will disappear more in the future.

"I think sleeping together is a great comfort for both of us. When he's asleep, I can pretend he's the husband without Alzheimer's." But she says even that part is getting difficult, because of the grief she feels when she wakes up.

"Every morning he's sad," my mother explained. "The first thing he does is look around for a while. Then when he gets up, I have to do everything for him. I'm hit with it right away. In fact, I do have to help him do pretty much everything and give him his pills. He can still shave, he can still brush his teeth, but after this restful time together, boom, right away, in the morning, you're faced with 'this is where we are.' You kind of sigh or take a deep breath and say, Well, here we go. The tasks that he is able to do for himself are fewer every day.

"I think I'm nearing the point that I am realizing that I have to save my life. This will involve his being taken care of during the day and then eventually he'll have to live someplace else. He can still feed himself; he can go to the bathroom by himself."

My mother says she doesn't think what she's doing is that extraordinary. "I'm fortunate to have a lovely family," she said, "and especially fortunate that he's loving and kind. It makes a lot of difference. He is polite; he wants to take my coat and pull out my chair. Many Alzheimer's patients are angry and lash out and are violent."

Looking back on their lives together, my mother said, "Taking care of Woody has become my life. I just hope I have the strength and the energy to develop my own life when he's gone. There will be a big hole. Most of my friends who are married would do the same thing I have done."

The exhaustion my mother and other caregivers experience isn't from the effects of Alzheimer's disease alone. It's from keeping up the pretense that their lives are normal, and from trying to pretend that he's okay and she's okay when neither of them is.

There are times, I am sure, that beyond the sorrow my mother feels about losing her spouse, she also feels like a failure. My father is not only unable to be the husband he once was, but he also can't even figure out which utensil to eat his food with. Every day he has to be told how to open the car door. Sometimes he emerges from the bedroom with his clothes on inside out. Each moment like this is an "in your face" demonstration, for my mother, of the fact that her world is falling apart.

A psychotherapist who specializes in treating the families of people who have Alzheimer's, Carolyn McIntyre, has identified what she terms the three stages of caregiving. In the early stage, she says, caregivers experience surprise, fear, denial, confusion, and sadness. In the middle stage they experience frustration, guilt, resentment, and conflicting demands. The late stage involves sadness, guilt, surrender, regrets, relief, solace, and closure.

One of the ways spouses and families can survive, McIntyre says, is to "honor the illness and keep it in its place. This means: don't be in denial. Make the necessary care changes in the family, but also don't go too far in giving up rituals and habits that allow joy and fun in the family."

When I came home, I wondered why my mother kept performing the same family rituals such as trying to maintain a social life with my father no matter how difficult it was—going to dinner, concerts, and church. I wondered, Why doesn't she just admit it's just too hard? Why not leave him home with me? Why doesn't she go do things alone?

Now, after being home and helping take care of my father for almost two years, I have come to understand why she continues to do everything from Christmas celebrations to Florida vacations. If she changed these rituals, changed their life together, and changed our family life, she would be resigning herself to this disease, even surrendering. She doesn't want to think of herself as someone apart from my father. Not yet anyway.

Chapter Six

Hospital Hell and Healing

In 2005 MY FATHER'S DOCTORS DECIDED HE needed knee replacement surgery. Not one, but two. And they decided it would be best to have them done at the same time. The idea of an Alzheimer's patient getting both knees replaced boggles the mind: getting ready for the trauma of surgery, the hospital experience itself, the months of physical therapy until he or she can walk normally again. It was something no spouse should have to handle alone. The idea of it made us all realize how difficult my mother's and father's situation had become. It was one of the reasons I had chosen to change my life to come home and help them.

Each day, my family talked about whether knee replacement surgery was the right thing to do. My older sister, Alison, said that not performing the surgery would be giving up on Dad, resigning him to a wheelchair, to inactivity, and that it may give him another reason to give up on life sooner than he needed to.

One friend said, "Don't do it!" He had seen people go through the pain of double knee replacement surgery and the weeks and months of physical therapy, without gaining any sort of substantial improvement in range of motion or use of their knees. He said the trauma of the surgery would do my father more harm than good. One of his friends who had gone through the surgery was never able to play tennis again.

But there is one thing that all of us who take care of my father have learned: It seems as though the more you can keep him, and I presume any Alzheimer's patient, connected and engaged, the more you can keep the effects of the disease at bay. If he could still walk or play tennis with his grandchildren, it would be worth it. We all agreed that being able to function with the full use of his legs would help to keep him participating in the world.

One thing that helped us remain united as a family about the surgery was that all the doctors involved in caring for my father felt it was a good idea, especially Dr. Rook, who had been treating Dad's knee problems for several years. The geriatric psychiatrist who treats him for Alzheimer's, Stephen Aronson, said that keeping up with the things he likes to do, such as tennis and other sports, would definitely help my father keep fighting the downward spiral of the disease. Dr. Aronson gave great support to the idea of double knee replacement surgery. So did my father's two general practitioners, Dr. White and Dr. Meri.

My father's knee doctor described his problem as "bone on bone." The cartilage had all but disappeared. Dad seemed to dread walking anywhere. I watched him begin shying away from doing almost any physical activity. He didn't even want to try playing tennis anymore. Mom's life was getting even more limited by his inability to walk for more than a few moments at a time. Air travel had become almost impossible, and going just about anywhere with Dad was exhausting. Just picking something up at the store with him was difficult. Whenever we entered a store, he asked to sit down. He began to ask if he could just sit in the car while my mother and I shopped and did errands.

Ultimately, we felt we had to treat Dad's physical problems as though he were a man without Alzheimer's. We asked ourselves, Wouldn't you want someone you love to have the best possible chance of physical improvement, even though the surgery and the ensuing physical therapy period would be difficult? My mother seemed to dread it, but felt strongly that it was the right thing to do. She made the final call and gave the green light.

As the day of the surgery drew near, it seemed as though there was a doctor's appointment every day. My sisters, my mother, and I were on the phone often, and we all knew we weren't just preparing for surgery. We were preparing for the very real possibility that Dad might not come back home. It wasn't just the general physical threat involved with any kind of major surgery. It was because we had heard about Alzheimer's patients who had simply lost their will to live while they were in the hospital. If all you have is the moment, and you have no memories, then the pain you are feeling at the moment is what you think life is like 24/7. You can't remember what it's like to feel healthy. That's why, it's believed, some Alzheimer's patients simply lose the will to live when they undergo painful surgery.

We wanted to do everything we could to remind Dad of life outside of the hospital and to remind him of who he was when he got out of surgery. I took pictures of the family and put them in frames so he'd have them in his hospital room. I found old photos and put together a photo album that he would have with him at the hospital. (I call it *The Book of Dad*.) It has pictures of him when he was a little boy, his mother and father, his whole family, his colleagues at his company, his singing group, family pets, and him when he served in the army overseas.

I went to a department store and found a Velcro paddle with a Velcro ball, so we could play catch and do hand–eye coordination exercises in the hospital room. I bought a portable CD player with headphones so he could listen to music in his hospital bed, and I began sorting through his CDs. I chose a lot of a capella music, his favorite Frank Sinatra and Ella Fitzgerald tunes, big band music, and of course CDs of his own singing group, the Grunyons.

My mother (the organized one) made sure all the paperwork was in order, including Dad's will. She and my father had already decided that if a disaster occurred in the operating room, he would not be resuscitated, and he had signed papers long ago that stated that he did not want to be kept alive by artificial means.

As my mother and I prepared for my father's surgery, I realized I had never focused this much on another person before. I remembered doing long-term special investigative reports on various topics from Malathion spraying in Los Angeles, to the U.S. Occupation of Haiti, to San Francisco's Municipal Railway System. I once lived for several days in a community in northern California that used only solar and wind power. I remembered getting ready each November for elections, and in particular, every four years when a presidential election occurred. So much of my life would revolve around this one event. I immersed myself in the topic, lived it, breathed it, and let it take over my life. Sometimes I didn't have time to eat or sleep, and I hardly noticed. All I cared about was The Big Story. But it had always been about work. This time my big project was a human being: my father.

I was beginning to understand how my friends who are mothers feel about their children, this total investment in someone else's life. Husbands and wives feel this when they take care of each other. My sisters and my mother were feeling it. A loved one needed them desperately, someone for whom they would drop everything. This was the kind of dedication and commitment I had experienced only briefly in my marriage and other relationships but then had fled from. (A friend of mine says of my marriage: "You stuck your big toe in, and then you pulled it back it out!" I was known for running.)

As I placed baby pictures of my father in his book, I thought how strange it was that I had chosen the other end of the spectrum. My friends were helping their children grow *into* the world. I was helping my father on his way *out of* this world.

It was the night before my father's surgery. My older sister arrived from Kalamazoo. My mother, my father, my sister, and I had dinner together. While we ate, I watched my father's eyes. I wanted his eyes to stay the way they were at that moment—untroubled, unaware of what was going to happen to him the next day.

We set our alarms for 5 a.m. None of us slept well except for Dad, who, as usual, slept through the entire night. When I woke up, I thought, There is one blessing that comes with Alzheimer's: he can't remember what he's been told will happen to him today.

I am sharing the story of my father's surgery and hospital stay partly because I want so much for the doctors and nurses and physical therapy specialists who helped him to know what a fantastic job most of them did. But I would also like anyone who has to take an Alzheimer's patient to a hospital for a major medical procedure to be warned about the difficulty they will face. I won't mince words here. Two weeks in the hospital and physical therapy afterward with an Alzheimer's patient was hell.

My older sister was extremely worried about the surgery, not because of what might happen with Dad's knees, not the loss of blood, not even the painful incision and the months of physical therapy. Her biggest concern was the potential for anxiety and fear and disorientation when he woke up and didn't know where he was or what was happening to him, and the potential impact of the anesthesia on Dad's already altered state of mind. She felt that one of us should be with him in the hospital twenty-four hours a day. The rest of the family agreed, and we talked with the hospital about this. My father's doctors arranged a plan with the hospital so that a family member could be with him throughout his stay.

My younger sister made plans to come with her family from West Virginia for the second week following the surgery. My older sister, who was starting a new semester teaching at Kalamazoo College, came to help in the first few days after surgery. With my mother, we scheduled what amounted to eight-hour shifts, with backup and on-call help at the ready from friends and members of my parents' church.

We continued to try to explain the surgery to my father up until the morning he went to the hospital, but no matter how we framed the process, he didn't really understand. "Why?" he would say. Then he would exclaim, "My knees are fine!" A woman at the Older Person's Commission where my father had been going to adult day care recommended that we not tell him about it until the day of the surgery. "He'll just get anxious," she said. It turns out that this is often the recommended route to take for Alzheimer's patients who are faced with traumatic events such as surgery. In their book *Alzheimer's A to Z*, Jytte Lokvig and John D. Becker describe the following scenario: "Your grandfather has to go to the hospital as an outpatient. To keep him from becoming unnecessarily anxious, wait until you're on the way to the hospital before you explain to him what's going to happen. He'll take his cues from your attitude and words. Stay calm and upbeat, but be straightforward and honest about what to expect, and then reassure him that you'll be there with him."

It turns out that quite a few experts agree about keeping Alzheimer's patients in the dark about future events they might not understand, especially painful ones such as surgery. But my family felt that it was wrong to keep information about upcoming surgery from my father. It felt condescending and patronizing, as if we were treating him like a child. My mother and I decided to talk about it openly in front of him and with him. His psychiatrist agreed. We always talked about it positively, telling him that soon he would have "new knees" and that he would be able to play tennis again by summertime.

The morning of the surgery, Dad seemed fine. Mom was worried and nervous, and so was my sister. I seemed to move into some sort of "zone" much the way I used to in radio when I covered a big story. I appeared calm on the outside and spoke in a calm voice the way I used to when I was reporting breaking news live on the radio or when I was anchoring a show, but inside, I soon realized,

I was a mess. As we walked toward the hospital door, I vomited on the lawn, right by the entrance to the hospital. It happened suddenly, very much the way it had happened when I was covering the school shootings at Columbine in April 1999. The similarity of my physical reaction to my father's upcoming trauma and my reaction to the school shootings stunned me.

Back then, KGO Radio flew me to Denver the night the shooting happened. I remember being in a kind of dream state as I drove from the airport in a rental car. When I got to the school, a news conference was already underway. The sense of tragedy ran deep. The revelation that two young high school students had planned and carried out the shooting had just come to light. Children and parents were crying all around me. Reporters surrounded the high school grounds. I remember a light snow on the ground. I did a string of live reports on KGO and began interviewing several people, including the chief of police. I walked back to my car holding my reporter pad, tape recorder, and microphone, and then, almost exactly like this moment at the hospital, I walked from the car door, headed to the curb, and threw up on the lawn. I went live on the radio again with another report ten minutes later.

As I did in my days as a reporter, I kept moving. Mom, Alison, and Dad had walked on ahead. As I had at Columbine, a few moments after I vomited, I walked through the automatic sliding doors into the hospital lobby and acted like nothing had happened.

From the moment we got inside the hospital, it was a nightmare. When we gave my father's name and announced what procedure he was scheduled for, the receptionist in the surgery waiting room sat my father in a wheelchair and tried to wheel him off alone, without my mother. My sister, mother, and I shouted, "Wait! Wait!" but she just kept going. Finally, one of us shouted, "Wait! We don't want him to be alone!" It was if she didn't hear us. She just kept going. As we discovered throughout our hospital experience, people seemed to be in a hurry. There were quite a few people in the waiting room, and one of us was forced to shout, "No, wait! He has Alzheimer's!"

It was just one of the many humiliations my father (and my family) would face over the next two weeks. Everyone in the waiting room turned to look at my father and at us. The receptionist who was wheeling Dad away seemed perturbed as she turned to my mother and said something like, "Oh, well, in that case, come on." That was that. My father and mother disappeared behind the hissing beige automatic doors as they closed. Already, we felt that there wasn't time or space in the system for someone afflicted with Alzheimer's. No thought seemed to be given to how to best deal with Alzheimer's patients.

My mother stayed with my father until he went into surgery. The process would involve replacing his arthritic knee joints with titanium and plastic. He would be given a general anesthetic. After the surgery, it would take him some time to come to.

The surgery took about four hours, and then my father had to stay in the recovery room for several more hours because of a development we did not foresee—a wildly erratic heartbeat. By the time my mother was allowed into post-op to see him, she says his jaw and his whole body were shaking. His skin looked blue. Was he shaking because of the cold in the recovery room where he had stayed longer than expected? Or was he shaking because he was afraid and alone and had no idea what was happening to him and no one was there during that critical period to comfort him? There he was, an Alzheimer's patient on a stretcher, his knees wrapped up, bleeding, hooked up to tubes and wires, completely alone.

Whatever the reason for his trembling, did he tell someone that he was cold? Did they see him trembling? Did they even notice? Did they try to make him warm? We will never know because, as with most Alzheimer's patients, it is almost impossible for Dad to articulate what he is experiencing or what has happened.

While we waited for my father to be stabilized, I asked several

hospital workers about the documented procedures for people
with Alzheimer's. It turns out there really weren't any. We learned
that only the people who read the charts would know that my father has Alzheimer's. That meant that the receptionists, the people
who would bring him his meals, all the "ancillary" people simply
wouldn't know about his disease, despite the fact that everything
they needed to do for with him would be affected by the disease,
everything from telling him to take his pills, to taking his temperature, to helping him to go to the bathroom, to feeding him. We
couldn't mandate that these people read his records. Nor could we
make sure a nurse or anyone else treating my father actually read
his chart. It was yet another reason to always have a family member
with him while he was in the hospital.

When we were finally able to join him in his hospital room,
after he was stabilized and recovering, he looked so pale. He had
gone from blue to a sort of sallow yellow. He continued to trem-
ble. His whole body shook. We asked for more blankets, but nothing seemed to keep him warm. As he started to come out of the
anesthesia, the doctor in charge of post-op said, "He seems confused about where he is." This was the one of the only times I can
remember losing control in the hospital. I said, "Of course he's
confused about where he is! He has Alzheimer's!" Actually, I sort
of shouted it, because at that moment everything about the hospital seemed insensitive to me.

As Dad's eyes fluttered open and he began to look at us, he
seemed to recognize my mother, my sister, and me. He didn't ask
many questions about what had happened. Of course, he was
groggy from the anesthetic, hardly able to speak. But I remember
one thing he said clearly as he surveyed the situation: "They took
me down."

I think this is an interesting statement, as in, They brought me
down. Indeed, in a way, they *did* "bring him down," as a man, as a
human being. He was felled like a tree in the forest.

He was also "taken down" the way a machine is taken down for repairs. I think that statement may have emanated from the part of Dad that was involved in engineering. He used to love talking about how machines worked and often talked to us about certain inventions he'd like to design. I think that, somewhere inside his Alzheimer's-afflicted brain, he knew that his body was an old, well-oiled machine, brought to a halt now for some major retooling.

When he said those words, I thought, Hopefully, after being "taken down," his legs will work better than they have in several years. Either that or he'll never be the same again, in his legs or in his head.

We would have to wait to find out what the result would be. We watched his eyes to see how much he knew about where he was, who he was, and what had happened to him, and whether he would be able to bounce back. My first impression as he tried to shake off the general anesthesia was that we had lost a lot of Dad in a matter of hours. I feared we might never get him back.

The first twenty-four hours after my father's knee replacement surgery are foggy for all of us. We'll never truly know what he endured. He was pale, confused, and unable to explain how he felt. He didn't seem to know what had happened to him. We explained the surgery with our usual enthusiasm, describing (over and over again) that he now had new knees, but somehow my father didn't share in the excitement. "What happened to my legs?" he would ask repeatedly. One of the few moments of levity for us the day after surgery was when he said, "Was all this really necessary?"

One of the biggest worries for the people taking care of him was that he would forget he had had major surgery and try to walk on his bandaged legs. Unfortunately, there is no way to *make* an Alzheimer's patient remember he's had surgery. The bed was equipped with an alarm system so that if he tried to climb out of bed, he would be caught in time by someone in the room or by a hospital worker in the hallway so that his "new knees" wouldn't be ruined. He wanted to get up constantly, and of course, he didn't understand why he couldn't walk on his legs.

Overnight, my father had suddenly come to look like a caricature of someone's grandmother. The orthopedic white stretch socks up over his knees and the flailing hospital gown that accidentally exposed his backside made him seem more frail and out of sync with the rest of the world than he already was. His hair was almost always askew, and it didn't seem like he would ever look like my dad again, much less act like him.

At some point, his pain seemed to get much worse. We asked what we could do, and a nurse finally told us that several hours had gone by since he had been given painkillers. We asked why. "Because he didn't ask for them," she said. "But he's got Alzheimer's!" we said. "He doesn't know how to ask for painkillers!" In fact, often, in order to be nice, if a nurse asked Dad if he wanted painkillers, he said, "No, but thank you for asking." He would wait for her to walk away, and then he would writhe in pain.

We realized we needed to start some sort of new plan for my father's stay in the hospital, such as giving him painkillers on a regular schedule whether he asks for them or not! Up to this point sometimes he got painkillers, and sometimes he didn't. We soon realized that whether he got the drugs he needed for pain regularly would depend on which nurses were working at the time and what shift the hospital was on.

The second day after surgery, Dad developed an infection. His white blood cell count was high, while his red blood cell count was very low, and he had a high fever. The doctor ordered two transfusions. He was losing a lot of blood, even though the blood he was losing from his knee operation was being recycled back into his bloodstream. Meanwhile, the doctors were simply unable to find the source of his infection. They treated him with antibiotics, but his temperature remained above normal.

The doctors finally decided to order an X ray of his lungs. I asked if I could go with him to the X-ray unit. A hospital worker said yes and wheeled Dad into the elevator, then left my father and me alone waiting in the hallway outside the X-ray room. The X-ray technician was conducting exams on several other patients. Finally, she emerged from the exam room, grabbed my father, and started trying to get him off the gurney to stand up on his legs. "Can he stand up?" she said. "No!" I shouted in an alarmed voice. "He's just had double knee replacement surgery!"

That moment struck fear in my heart. What if someone hadn't been there with my father? Would the X-ray technician have called someone upstairs to find out if my father could stand up on his bandaged knees, or would she have attempted to get Dad into a standing position only to have him crumple to the ground, injuring himself and undoing the expensive surgery and thousands of dollars worth of care? Apparently, she had not read Dad's chart. She didn't know he had had double knee replacement surgery, and she didn't know he had Alzheimer's.

The technician wheeled Dad into the X-ray room and began to ask him to move his arms into different positions. He couldn't understand some of the commands, and he was foggier than usual due to the drugs and the trauma of being in the hospital. In the end, I helped him perform some of the tasks necessary to achieve successful X rays. The entire event made me realize how vulnerable my father was and how much someone like him needs an advocate. All hospital patients who are mentally impaired in some way are at an extreme disadvantage if they don't have an advocate with them constantly.

The doctor told us that the X rays revealed a small infection in one of my father's lungs, which was a bit frightening for all of us since he was seventy-eight years old. The elderly are considered very susceptible to lung infections and pneumonia, especially in the hospital. He was given more antibiotics and started to improve immediately. After three days, the doctors decided that my father was well enough to be moved into the physical therapy unit.

The night before my father was moved into physical therapy, I watched him with such admiration. Despite all the confusion and chaos, and the incredible pain he was obviously experiencing, Dad thanked the nurses each time they left his room, even if they had caused him more pain by drawing blood or giving him a shot. He was disoriented, and he often hallucinated in the night. In his sleep, he moved his hands around like fluttering birds, and he talked out loud, almost always uttering positive, optimistic statements. Sometimes at 3 or 4 a.m. he would say loudly and clearly, "Thank you!" or "Wonderful!" One night, after a grueling and painful day, he fell into a deep sleep. I heard a kind of moaning from his hospital bed. I thought he was groaning from the pain, but the sound turned into singing, and I realized he was singing in perfect tenor harmony the song "Now the Day Is Over." It's a hymn my mother and father and I had been singing a lot together since I had come home. We always sing the first verse:

> Now the day is over
> Night is drawing nigh
> Shadows of the evening
> Steal across the sky

When he had finished singing the song, and still in a very deep sleep, he said in a loud voice, "Rosemary, you made my life. Thank you." There was a pause, and then he said, "You make the whole world possible."

Then his snoring started again.

One night, two nurses entered his hospital room, flicking on the fluorescent lights in a rush of activity and waking my father from a deep and drugged sleep. They said in a loud and cheerful tone, "Time to take your pills!" My father tried to leap out of bed (forgetting he had just had both of his knees replaced in a painful and difficult surgery just a few days ago) and said "What? It's time to pay my bills?" and tried to search frantically for his wallet. Of course, he set off the alarms on the side of his bed and ripped himself out of various devices he was plugged into. More nurses came running.

You have to be able to laugh at incidents like this. It is the only way to survive the situation. But it shouldn't have happened this way.

Let's step back a minute and examine what's going on: He's on massive amounts of drugs including pain pills and sleeping pills. He's just had both knees replaced. He's got wires and tubes coming out of him. He's got Alzheimer's. He's in bed with an alarm that will go off and alert the whole floor when he tries to jump out of bed, which he does on a regular basis, since, because he's got Alzheimer's, he can't remember he just had knee surgery, much less where he is. And yet nurses were flying in and out of his room at all hours of the night, with no warning, flicking on the lights and shouting. It was traumatic almost every time they came in the room. Were they in a hurry? (That must be the reason, I thought.) My father was confused. Of course, because he had Alzheimer's, he didn't know why he was being accosted with blood pressure machines, thermometers, a painful catheter, and other tubes inserted into his veins.

To be fair, not all the nurses woke him up in this shocking manner. Some were gentle and tried to wake him slowly, and some didn't even need to turn on the lights. Some did what they had to do gently, quietly, and in darkness, or in the dimmest possible light, but they were the exceptions, not the norm. The majority of the time, it was as if he were under assault. It was particularly disruptive in the night. The nurse assaults seemed to vary in intensity from day to day. Perhaps it depended on how busy the nurses were, whether they had the luxury of slowly and quietly waking up the patient so as not to cause further psychic damage, or whether they needed to get the job done quickly, and thus intensely and insensitively. The only excuses I could come up with were lack of time and a completely callous attitude. I wanted to believe it was the former and not the latter.

Unfortunately, some of the nurses who *did* have time didn't seem to understand about Alzheimer's. One spoke baby talk to my father and pinched his cheeks—my father, the CEO of a company who served on several committees, a graduate of U of M, a pillar of the Detroit business community. And here is a nurse pinching his cheeks, saying, "Woody, Woody, Sweet Woody" in baby talk, her face pressed up against his as though he were a tiny child. It must have been a nightmare for him (it was for me, just watching it). As if he already didn't feel as though he were on another planet, now this woman he didn't know was pressing her face against his and speaking gibberish!

I know it must be tedious to have to tell the same patient over and over again how to lift his tongue for the thermometer, that he must lift the glass to his lips to drink the water to swallow his pills, why he has to have a shot, and, repeatedly, not to take his catheter out. Perhaps pretending he was a child helped them to not become impatient with him. Maybe that was the reason for the baby talk. But my father is not a child. He is an adult, and he deserves to be treated like an adult, even though he's an adult with Alzheimer's. I know nurses have some of the most difficult jobs in the universe, and they are underpaid and overworked. Yet wouldn't they want their parent, or anyone they loved, to be treated with grace and re-spect and dignity?

My older sister, Alison, my mother, my younger sister, Libby, and I took turns staying overnight with my dad. We took copious notes during our shifts.

We wanted to figure out why the experience was so traumatic, and what could be done to make it less so. Then again, maybe being in a hospital is traumatic for everyone, no matter how hard the nurses and doctors try to make it better.

The period after the surgery was grueling. My sisters had to return to work and their families. Sensing my mother's fatigue and lack of sleep, I took the night shifts to give her relief. Finally, we looked into hiring a night sitter from an agency. It didn't go well. In fact, there were conflicts between the agency-hired nurse and the hospital nurses. It caused so many problems that we let her go after one night, and I went back on the overnight shift. Only after my father was released from the hospital did we learn that the hospital would have provided night sitters free of charge.

No matter how hard we tried to soften the blow to my dad of undergoing surgery, physical therapy, and two weeks in the hospital, he must have experienced a great deal of confusion, chaos, and pain during this difficult time.

The first time Dad went to physical therapy in the hospital, my mother went with him. At first, it seemed to go quite well, despite some misunderstandings about directions—misunderstandings that come with the territory if you are a patient with Alzheimer's. For some reason, however, many people who worked with my father were not even informed that he had the disease.

My father, who is very perceptive about the way people regard him, felt very much "under the microscope" throughout his hospital stay. He often trembled when asked to perform certain tasks, as if they were tests he could fail. When we took him to physical therapy, he felt like it was something he could win or lose, with possible negative consequences, instead of an exercise that was supposed to help his knees work better. On one of the first trips to physical therapy, when he still didn't understand why he was being asked to perform certain tasks, unfortunately, a visiting RN came to observe. When Dad was told to raise his arms and then place his hands on his shoulders, he didn't understand the directions (as happens with many Alzheimer's patients). Instead, he put his hands behind his ears. It looked rather awkward, especially since none of the other patients were holding their hands in that spot.

My father was shaking throughout the process. To make matters worse, my mother said the visiting RN pointed at my father, and shouted, "Oh, look at him! He has his hands behind his ears!" and started laughing. My mother said my father turned red and knew that he was being ridiculed. After that he trembled even more.

As my mother explains, someone in my father's position is going through so much already that, in addition to all the other physical and mental assaults he must endure, he shouldn't be ridiculed. My mother told the doctor in charge of physical therapy what had happened. He was upset about it, and he apologized. He promised that something like this would not occur again under his watch. Lessons learned. For all of us.

After doing the first series of exercises, my father was supposed to learn to use a walker. First, as would happen with any Alzheimer's patient, he had no idea what a walker was. (Why didn't we practice using a walker with him before he underwent surgery? I have no idea.) When he did figure out what it was used for, he was appalled! A walker? Woody Geist with a walker? We all saw his sense of pride emerge. For some reason, he had enough cognition to equate the walker with something he perceived as a weakness.

"I don't need this! What is this for?" he said, incredulous, when his physical therapist brought the walker in. He almost scoffed. He said those words over and over again whenever the nurses or physical therapy specialists slid the contraption up to this bed. Sometimes, when the nurses weren't around, he would lean over to me and say in whisper, "Just don't tell them! I'm going to the bathroom without it!" Of course, when he would try to do so, all the alarms would go off again. It became like a Laurel and Hardy comedy show—my father, with his hospital gown flailing open behind him, hobbling to the bathroom with his white bandaged legs, the alarms going off, and the nurses running to respond. This was the daily routine. The folks in physical therapy tried to explain to him repeatedly the importance of the walker, that it would help his legs heal from the surgery. It just didn't work.

Finally, several days after the surgery, Dad began to understand that he was supposed to use the walker whenever he went *anywhere*. It had finally sunk in. "This?" he would say, pointing at the walker as if it were a living thing. "Yes, this!" we would say, over and over again. Sometimes he actually remembered and sort of weakly pushed the contraption in front of him, but most of the time he didn't.

As has happened often throughout my father's disease, he came to his own conclusion about his surroundings and how to manage them. He decided to drag the walker behind him. That's when we knew his legs were getting better. That's also when we knew Dad was a man who would make his own rules, even though he had Alzheimer's. Using a walker just might not be the best way to go for him, we thought. In fact, when I look back on it now, skipping it altogether might have been the best route for him, and maybe for almost any other Alzheimer's patient who has both knees replaced.

Between sessions of learning to change his clothes without hurting his new knees, relearning to brush his teeth and comb his hair and get to the bathroom on his own, performing his arm exercises (the usual physical therapy one goes through for double knee replacement surgery), drinking chocolate Ensure with ice, eating lots of overcooked vegetables and macaroni and cheese, we did the following:

> We watched a lot of CNN.
> We saw lots of Fred Astaire movies on TNT.
> We watched reruns of football games that happened
>   long ago but were new to him.
> He listened to lots of music on his CD player.
> We sang lots of his favorite songs.
> We read him the *New York Times*.
> We played catch with the Velcro ball and Velcro
>   paddles.
> We visited with friends and relatives who came to the
>   hospital to see him.

Somehow, Dad survived his two-week hospital stay. The color started coming back into his face. He even smiled again. But at the end of the day, I feel there's got to be a better way. If you are a caregiver for an Alzheimer's patient who must go into the hospital, I have a few suggestions:

- Talk with everyone in the hospital about the disease. Ask how the administrators can make sure that all the nurses and doctors treating him know he's got Alzheimer's and what he can and can't do on his own.
- If you, as a family, can work out ways for one of you to be with the patient for twenty-four hours a day, do it.
- Make a book of his life filled with photos to show him repeatedly and remind him of all the people in his life.
- Have pictures of the family (make sure he's in the picture with his family members, if possible) in frames to put around the hospital room.
- Bring a CD player and headset and a bunch of his favorite CDs.
- Have a hand–eye coordination device, tool, or sport on hand, such as Velcro paddles with Velcro balls, or other games that you can play with in the hospital room without breaking things.
- Bring some hand-stress balls so he can flex his hands often in the hospital room.
- Do various wooden and jigsaw puzzles with him.
- Finally, don't be afraid to talk with doctors and nurses about your concerns.

In the book *Alzheimer's A to Z*, authors Jytte Lokvig and John D. Becker suggest having the word *ALZHEIMER'S* written big and bold on the cover of the patient's chart. Hospital officials told us that "privacy rules" prevented them from giving this information to all who dealt with my father. Yet it seems like common sense. Alzheimer's is a medical condition—important information that should always be on every chart or order. An example of that was what happened to my father in the X-ray room.

Lokvig and Becker write, "Amazingly, hospital personnel are often not prepared to handle special situations like dementia and Alzheimer's. You will want to stop anyone in their tracks if they start using baby talk." They suggest that you ask hospital staff to explain medical procedures in a step-by-step normal tone of voice and repeat the details as often as necessary.

I wish I had read this book before my father had gone to the hospital. Baby talk was used all too often by several staff members during his hospital stay. It offended me as well as my mother. And if it offended *us*, I can't even imagine how my father felt about it. Sadly, baby talk is how many people who take care of Alzheimer's patients communicate with them. As the aforementioned book suggests, you have every right to ask anyone who spends time with your loved one to treat him or her with respect, like an adult, and you have the right to ask them *not* to use baby talk.

After the surgery and almost two weeks of physical therapy in the hospital, my father finally came home. Once he got home, the doctor ordered physical therapy three times a week to get his new knees in proper working order. He had blood drawn twice a week to check his Coumadin and white blood cell levels. Because the blood draws took place in the hospital where he had had his knee replacement operation, one day I decided to take him to the physical therapy floor where he had spent those harrowing two weeks after his surgery. I knew it could be a risk. If he didn't remember it, it could upset him to have people fawning all over him and not be able to figure out why. If the sight of the place did cause him to remember physical therapy, would it be a good thing to help him recall such a painful and traumatic chapter in his life?

We got out of the elevator on the fourth floor where his

physical therapy had taken place. When we came up to the automatic doors that led to the hallway where his room was, he said, "Uh-oh." I said, "Dad, do you remember being here?" He said without hesitating, "Yes, I do." It was the first time he had acknowledged any memory of the surgery or the ensuing physical therapy. He looked in the room where his physical therapy had taken place every day. One of the therapists who had worked with Dad saw him and shouted, "Oh my god! I can't believe it!" Dad was walking straight and true and beautifully that day. It made me realize how far Dad had come, and that all our work was actually paying off. I hoped he would realize it, too, on some level. The therapist was extremely impressed with how well Dad was walking. He found two of the nurses who had worked with him through those long days and nights. They hugged my father, and he seemed to remember them. We had him walk down the hall while the staff watched. Some of the nurses clapped and cheered. They thanked us for coming. As we left, Dad was smiling, but he looked a little confused.

When we got in the elevator and the doors swooshed shut, Dad said, "What was that all about? Did I almost die or something?"

Chapter Seven

Helping Hands

BEING IN THE HOSPITAL WITH MY FATHER during his knee operation was like being in a very dark tunnel and not knowing whether we would—or could—ever get to the other side. When we finally got home, it was as if the three of us had to learn how to live by new post-hospital rules. My father had forgotten a lot of the daily rituals he used to know. We had to teach him where things were in the house, how to brush his teeth, how to shave, how to comb his hair, and how to take his pills on a daily basis. My mother and I had to learn how to live with a person who now needed constant care and comfort as well as physical therapy. We realized *we* needed comfort, too.

My mother and I learned many lessons both while my father was in the hospital and after he got out. One of the most important lessons was that caregivers need to share their pain. Perhaps more than anything, they need someone to help them out when they can't take it anymore.

It seems to me you build your own networks. You find people who have the same philosophy about Alzheimer's, and you go from there. Ultimately, my mother has developed a support group of friends, the church, and the community around her. Since I came home, we support each other in these strange new roles we have taken on.

Outside of our family, the church has been most helpful to us, especially when Dad was in the hospital and undergoing physical therapy after his surgery. I realized how strong my father is during those two weeks in the hospital, and what grace there is to this man. I also realized what a brave, strong, and organized woman my mother is, and how weak I am.

Being in a hospital is exhausting, even when you're not the patient. It was hard enough for me to deal with the noises, the alarms, the nurses coming in and out, the bizarre and unnatural routines of the day. I kept wondering how Dad, an Alzheimer's patient, was processing all of this. He asked where he was constantly. He continually asked what had happened to him. He had to deal with lights, shots, pain, drugs, and alarms going off on his bed when he'd forget he'd had the knee surgery. He hallucinated often. I felt completely helpless, unable to make him feel better.

Just when it seemed that I and other family members who were staying with him in the hospital were ready to break, rescuers appeared from my mother and father's congregation. They always seemed to arrive just in time.

They belong to the choir at our church, and I call them the Pageturners, because several of them stand next to my father in choir and turn the pages so that he can continue to sing in the tenor section. Because of the Pageturners, and the patience of Nancy, the choir director, my father and mother have been able to go to choir rehearsals and sing in the choir on Sundays, even as his disease has gotten progressively worse.

Dad often remembers his part and the words. But if there's a new piece of music to learn, the Pageturners have even more work to do to help him rehearse and perform. They never complain, even though I know it must have a negative impact on their choir experience. Bobbie and Mary Louise are the two who stand next to Dad, but the rest of the church members have been turning pages for my father and our entire family, in ways big and small, for quite some time.

Mary Louise, Jim, Chris, Arlene, Ralph, the minister Leonetta, and many more all showed up at the hospital to help take care of Dad for an hour or two at a time so the rest of us could get away for lunch or dinner or just to take short breaks—to exercise or just to breathe. Members of the church sent cards and prayers throughout the ordeal and lit candles for Dad at Sunday services. Sometimes they just came to hold Dad's hand while he slept so we could get away from time to time. When my father finally came home from the hospital, he was, once again, able to stand next to Mary Louise and Bobbie in the tenor section of the choir on Sunday mornings. Throughout this ordeal, my family has learned that there are people everywhere, waiting to turn the pages for you so you can keep singing.

Despite my father's relatively speedy recovery, and even with all the help we received, we faced another problem. A month after the double knee replacement surgery, my father began to wake up every morning saying, "I'm dead." During the day, when my mother and I would ask him how he felt, he would say, "I'm dying." Sometimes he sat in a chair with his head in his hands.

He had gone through so much in surgery. He had done so well in physical therapy. So many had helped him recover. My mother had worked so hard to coordinate everything and make sure he had the best possible postsurgery scenario. And now he seemed to have lost his will to live.

It all seemed so sad, as if everything we had done had been completely useless. All the pain my father had gone through in surgery and in physical therapy seemed to have been for nothing. Sometimes he said he wanted to shoot himself. He wasn't eating. He had lost a significant amount of weight in the hospital, and now he wasn't gaining it back. In fact, he had lost even more weight since he had gotten home.

This made my mother and me, who were supposed to be his caregivers, his nourishers, feel as though we had done something wrong. In those darks days all three of us felt we had failed. My father most likely felt like he had failed as a human being because he couldn't remember things and couldn't help us with anything. My mother felt like she had failed as a wife because she couldn't make him feel better. And I felt I had failed at one of the tasks that had prompted me to come home. A cloak of depression seemed to billow and surround all of us.

I had gotten into the habit of taking Dad to the gym about fifteen minutes from our home to do physical therapy. At this point, he could also spend about ten minutes hitting the ball back over the net on the tennis court. Sometimes we would work out on the machines. The physical therapists had taught me the proper routines, and I had become adept at exercising his knees. He could also spend about ten minutes on the stationary bicycle. Then, after we worked out (this was his favorite part), we'd sit in the Jacuzzi. He calls it "the hot place." Whenever he sat down in "the hot place," he smiled, but when we got out of the Jacuzzi, the smiles were few and far between.

My mother and I tried everything to improve his mood and his appetite, but nothing seemed to work. His mood did not get better, nor did his appetite. One day I struck up a conversation with a young woman at a café about trying to help my father gain a few pounds. In the middle of discussing how to make an extremely caloric milkshake for my father, she took a deep breath and looked me in the eye, as if she were measuring me for something. Then she said, "You know the best thing for depression and lack of appetite is marijuana."

It was an interesting notion. I asked her more about it and wondered how I could get some without breaking the law. Despite the fact that my father had smoked three packs of Kents a day in the 1950s, I somehow couldn't picture him lighting up a joint. Besides, the idea of an Alzheimer's patient messing with matches, combustible material, papers, and smoke is not advisable.

The woman told me that the best way for an Alzheimer's patient to take marijuana is to ingest it, for instance, in brownies. Then she stopped again, paused, and looked at me. There was a moment of silence. Finally, she said, "Look, we bake on Fridays." Marijuana brownies! Pickup time, she said, was Friday afternoon. For a moment, I thought about it. Then the picture formed in my mind of me in my car with the out-of-state license plates, pulled over on the side of the road, a plate of marijuana brownies on the seat next to me, telling the officer that I was merely doing my Friday afternoon pickup of marijuana brownies for my ailing father. Hmmm.

My mother said it was okay to call my father's internist to discuss his mood and appetite problem and find out what he thought about the marijuana idea. Dad's doctor said he could prescribe Marinol, which is a legal form of marijuana. My understanding of the drug is that it retains positive aspects of marijuana, mainly the influence on mood and appetite. We picked up a bottle of sixty pills from the local pharmacy the next day and began giving them to Dad before lunch and dinner. They are like small pearls— strange, round things. Dad rolled the first one around in the palm of his hand and then lobbed it into his mouth with the chocolate milk we had given him to wash it down.

After a couple of days, we began to see a change. His appetite started to get better. He began to finish his meals, instead of stirring or stabbing at the food with utensils and saying he wasn't hungry.

We decided then that the rest of Dad's meds probably needed adjustment after the trauma of the knee replacement surgery. We took him to see his geriatric psychiatrist, Dr. Stephen Aronson, who specializes in cognitive disorders. Just being with him cheered Dad up considerably. Dr. Aronson repeated his mantra: "Play to your strengths." We all talked about the importance of physical activity and using Dad's new knees as much as possible: tennis, golf, going out to dinner, too—whatever Dad felt strong enough to do.

Dr. Aronson also adjusted Dad's cocktail of pills. We were a little wary of adding more prescriptions to an already loaded pill box, but Dad's talk of dying and death and the way he was hanging his head in the wake of his surgery made us feel that trying almost anything to improve his mood and inspire him to continue with physical therapy and the healing process in his knees was imperative. So Dr. Aronson added Wellbutrin, an antidepressant, to his medications.

The Wellbutrin took a few days to work, but then it was a different world. Dad woke up one morning before Mom did, showered and shaved by himself, and went out to get the newspaper without being reminded to do so. One morning I woke up early to go bird-watching. I was walking down the dirt road in front of our house, and I saw a tall figure strolling to the newspaper box in the distance. I wondered who that person could be, and then I realized it was Dad. I got tears in my eyes. The month before, I didn't think we'd get to this point. There were times I didn't know whether he'd walk again.

That morning, for the first time in several weeks, Dad didn't talk about dying. He even smiled. He ate his whole breakfast. It was like he was "on" again. He wasn't "checking out" the way he'd been doing since he got home from the hospital. It was as if he could hear what I was saying again. He was participating with us, participating in life again. It was almost eerie. He had bounced back again. I thought, Dad is back. Who knows how long this will last? However long it does, I'm going to enjoy these moments. I know this may be fleeting, but it could be more than just a few days we've gained here. It could be a few months.

That evening, I put two big chocolate chip cookies and milk next to him and he ate both cookies and drank all the milk. Highly unusual. For a moment, I thought, Is this "the munchies" from the Marinol?

It's as if we finally got the mix right, thanks to doctors who were willing to think outside the box and not give up on Dad. This was the best he'd been, mentally and physically, in months. Here's what my father was taking at the time:

Reminyl: 12 mg twice a day
Lexapro: 40 mg twice a day
Namenda: 10 mg twice a day
Aricept: 10 mg once a day
Ritalin: 20 mg once a day
Marinol: 2.5 mg twice a day (as needed)
Wellbutrin: 150 mg once a day
Remeron: 45 mg once a day
Isoptin: 120 mg once a day

One of the biggest lessons we had learned from this stage of my father's recovery from surgery and from his disease is that one must fight to get the mix of meds right. One must fight for the comfort, happiness, and health of a person living with Alzheimer's. We'd done a pretty good job of fighting for what was best for my father up to this point. All we could do now was keep our fingers crossed, and surround him with love.

Chapter Eight

Whistling in the Dark

It was the morning of August 17, 1977. My father was planted at his usual place at the table at the summer cottage, eating breakfast. He unfolded the newspaper and exclaimed, "Oh my God! Elvis Presley died! And he died 'straining at song'!" Someone asked, "Straining at song? How can that be?" One of us grabbed the paper from my father and read it. "No, Dad, it was straining a *stool*, not straining at song!"

We laughed very hard. Not at Elvis's death, mind you, or the way he died. We were laughing at my father's mistake. We were laughing at the fact that my father, once again, had given music special powers, as he always had. Perhaps that's when we realized music was so important to him he thought it could give someone life, and take it away.

You know all the clichés: Music lifts you up. Music fills your heart. Music makes the world go 'round. But for my father, in the late stages of Alzheimer's, it is more than that. Music makes him come alive.

Sometimes, especially when we're having a bad day during which my dad can't understand words or identify objects, and when he seems to be moving slowly, as if his batteries have run out, I lead him to a large mirror. I did this a lot before he sang with his a cappella singing group at his eightieth birthday party. We both stand directly in front of the mirror so we can watch our faces as we sing, and then I start singing a song he used to perform on a regular basis, preferably one in which he had a solo. "Shooby-doin'," a jazz tune written by Johnny Mercer, was one of his most beloved solos with the twelve-man singing group he'd performed with for forty years.

When I begin singing the song, often less than one word or bar into it, he chimes right in with his part and all the lyrics. At first, though, he stands in a slouched position with his head bent down, not looking at himself in the mirror. After the first few verses, pointing to the mirror, I say, "Look, Dad!" Sometimes I reach over and gently tilt his head and body a bit so he'll turn toward the mirror and stand the way he would during a performance. At my urging, he starts watching himself sing as he looks in the mirror, and that is when something remarkable happens. He stands up straighter, looking directly into the mirror as if he were on stage. I can see his face change as if some sort of lucidity and understanding has floated into the room, introduced by music. As he sings and looks into the mirror, he seems to remember the man he once was—the man who couldn't wait to take the stage to sing with the Grunyons or in a musical; the man who stood up tall and straight with arms outstretched looking up at the ceiling as he hit a high note; the man who ran a company and sat behind a big wooden desk, who gave speeches and took initiative and took control.

As I watch the two of us singing together in the mirror, it's almost eerie, as though someone else has taken over his body. Essentially that *is*, kind of, what occurs. Someone without Alzheimer's—the old Woody—appears. "Muscle memory" is what people call it. The music seems to cue him, wake him up, and take him back to the time before the Alzheimer's plaque set in, to the time when he remembered everything. Then he starts moving like he used to move, smiling like he used to smile. He even starts making facial expressions the way he used to make them when he sang with the

Grunyons, even if the meaning of the words he is singing may now elude him.

Dad's newfound presence lasts the duration of the song. He hits the final note looking triumphantly into the mirror. Then the minute the song is over, he whistles nervously and starts curling in on himself again, slouching over. It's almost as if he deflates, as if the song never happened.

One day when we finished singing, I could tell he didn't really remember what he had just done. He looked a bit stunned and unsure of what had just occurred, and then he looked in the mirror with his watery-blue eyes and said, "Who is that guy?"

Why can't the impact music has on him be inserted into the rest of his brain cells and body? Why can't the singing Woody stay with him throughout the rest of the day? Nietzsche said, "We listen to music with our muscles." Clearly these muscles continue to work in my father even as Alzheimer's takes everything else away.

Dr. Lola Cuddy is professor emeritus in the Department of Psychology at Queen's University in Ontario and director of the Music Cognition Laboratory, which she founded in 1965. Her main field of research is music perception and cognition. She is the editor of the journal *Music Perception* and has received many grants and awards. Most recently, Dr. Cuddy, along with coinvestigators Dr. Jackie Duffin and Dr. Sudeep Gill, was awarded a Grammy Foundation Award for research on Alzheimer's disease and music.

I asked Dr. Cuddy to explain why people like my father can remember the words and music to almost all the songs they'd ever sung when everything else seems to have fallen away.

"Scientific research does not yet have an answer to this question," she replied. "I would be very cautious about any claims here. We do not know, for instance, whether any other skills might also be preserved in some individuals. We have heard of preserved skills at domino and bridge. If so, that would mean that music does not have a special status, but rather that it shares preservation with some overlearned 'meaningful' skills. However, a case for a special status for music is still possible: music and speech engage different brain structures and music may be tied more to primitive emotional brain processes than is, say, object recognition. So it may be that there are specially preserved networks in the brain for music."

Dr. Cuddy explained, "It appears that the brain processes dedicated to music have often been spared in Alzheimer's disease and other forms of memory impairment. Music memory has a special cognitive status that may allow it in many cases to remain immune to even the wide-reaching and devastating effects of dementia. This preservation could serve as an important avenue to enhanced quality of life for those who have lost so many other abilities. A subsequent step is to understand how caregivers, family members, and friends might use this information to employ music in a variety of beneficial ways. Music may entertain or soothe an individual and may also assist emotional communication between individuals. In other words, it may provide a route for human contact when other routes are no longer available."

As Dr. Cuddy mentioned, it is not only that music is retained in Alzheimer's patients, but also that music may even help implant memories in people who suffer from dementia and Alzheimer's.

It's hard to find research that explains the deep imprint music seems to have on my father's soul, and the way his passion for it has endured the ravages of his disease. I believe the power of music propels my father through the plaque in his brain. I believe it helps him leap across neurotransmitters into the lucid world, even if only for a few moments. I believe that music can even mask the fact—for him and for us—that he is "broken inside."

For people like my father, who comes alive when he sings, music is a comfort, a kind of company, a reminder, a way to explain things that those of us in the non-Alzheimer's world will never understand. I am convinced that music is a road back to the world people with

Alzheimer's once lived in—a road back to friends, family, husbands, wives, children, and grandchildren. Music provides a way back in to life and love for people living with Alzheimer's.

My father has been singing since he was a little boy. His father played the piano, and there were several singers and performers in his family. It isn't clear how anyone found out Woody could sing when he was so young, but my grandmother took him to Grosse Pointe Memorial Church where a well-known choir director, Malcolm John, took him under his wing. My grandmother told us he was just six years old when he joined the choir. Little Woody wound up recording a solo on an LP (they had records back then, and I remember this one had a burgundy label) of "Lullay Thou Little Tiny Child," a Christmas hymn, and several other songs. He sang solos at the church on Sundays and performed at various venues in the Detroit area. I have listened to several records and tapes from this time in his life, and on the recordings, my father's voice is clear, sweet, and strong.

I am not sure my father had a happy childhood, especially after his family lost everything during the Depression years. I think music took him away from his family in a good way and gave him an identity of his own. It provided a place for him to go where he felt he belonged. From what my father used to tell me, music made him feel special. He seemed to embrace the identity of a singer more than any other in his life—more than that of basketball and tennis star in high school, or graduate of U of M, or even president of his company.

Mike Mitchell, a choral conductor and professor of music at Oakland University explains: "It all goes back to the human voice. This is the music that's made by our bodies. So no two sounds, no two human voices, are alike in their natural state. This is the most visceral and completely human sound. There's lots of great music in the world that's not made by the human voice. But for me that's what it goes back to, that's where it starts, that's the basis for it: the human voice."

Professor Mitchell says people who sing in choirs, and particularly a cappella groups, develop a special bond. He describes the lifelong friendships of people who've sung together in choruses, and he says there is a unique intimacy that occurs when people harmonize with each other. "I think the blending of human voices is a special sound. I think the blending of any set of musical instruments is something special. But one of the things that is unique to these a cappella groups is that one of the goals when they sing together is to blend perfectly. So the idea is that the human voice can be manipulated to make different kinds of sounds, and that when these a cappella groups get together and sing, one of the things they want to achieve through the group from guy to guy to guy is that they sound the same. That's what's called blend and/or balance, where one guy isn't louder than the other. The overtones produced by the human voice itself are unique, and when you put them together, you get a set of overtones."

Professor Mitchell has seen people become transformed by the choral experience. He still carries a picture in his wallet of the time he feels his life was changed when he won a singing competition with an a cappella group in high school. He continues to be in touch with several chorus members from that era in his life.

This kind of singing may have been a way for my father—raised in the '30s, coming of age in the '40s—to have intimate relationships with other men in an era when that could happen only by playing sports or singing. So why does my father remember all the words and parts to almost every song he's ever sung even as his disease progresses? Professor Mitchell says, "Maybe in his soul— what's inside him—that's who he really was. Of course he was all those other things, but at the most basic level, he was a musician." Professor Mitchell adds, "Some people are never lucky enough to find that."

After he married my mother, my father joined a barbershop quartet. It was one of the only musical experiences my mother can remember that he didn't embrace with complete joy. Though my father enjoyed the ringing harmonies, as I recall, the lack of subtlety of barbershop and particularly the matching outfits many groups wore (his own group, called the Four Baritones, refused to wear matching clothes) just weren't right for him. A music professor at Oakland University, Wally Collins, heard my father sing and asked him to audition for a twelve-man singing group called the Grunyons, which had been performing in the Detroit area for several years.

In his thirties and forties, my father decided to sing not only with the Grunyons, but also with the church choir. When I was in elementary and junior high school, he also performed with the local theater group called the Avon Players. I remember being shocked one time when I saw him performing in the musical *Kiss Me Kate*. He serenaded a woman on a balcony from the stage. I thought when I saw him in front of the audience that he would be the epitome of suave and debonair. But when I saw him on stage, he was wearing a green floppy hat with a feather in it and green tights that made his legs look even skinnier than they already were. Yet when he sang, his voice rang through the theater in a smooth and commanding way. Just as they had in college whenever they heard him sing, women swooned.

I believe my father's authentic self resides in music.

I interviewed Dick Bourez, one of my father's best friends for almost four decades. They are both baritones in the Grunyons. Dick remembers when my father first discovered that he might have Alzheimer's. "He was very open about it," Dick said. "He would laugh about it—his problems and his memory." Dick said that at first, it wasn't really noticeable, but several years into the disease, the repeated questions, which are a signature behavior of people with Alzheimer's, became more pronounced. "He would ask me, 'Where are we going?' And I'd tell him. That would happen every ten minutes. 'Where are we going tonight?' I'd answer. Then he'd ask it again."

Like other people I've talked with about my father, Dick believes my father's optimism has helped him survive. "He never had a negative attitude towards it," Dick said. "He understood the disease I think, and he made the best of it. He never felt sorry for himself. He could laugh at himself. And he loved sports. The physical shape he was in I think helped him a lot mentally. He used to look forward to playing tennis all the time, especially with his grandsons. He stayed physically fit. I don't think he was constantly thinking about Alzheimer's. He was looking at the positive things in life and the things he could still take part in. With the Grunyons, even in his last years of actively singing, he was learning the new music. He couldn't order from a menu in a restaurant. He'd have difficulty, but somehow or other, he was able to read and learn the new music, whether he was hearing it from somebody else singing or listening to tapes. He had so many friends. And he was just a real joy to be around."

I asked Dick to tell me more about what may now be termed the "male bonding" of the Grunyons.

"We were all pretty much the same age, and we all had children about the same age," Dick said. "When I joined, our families and our kids all knew each other. We are all really one big family. We were aware of everybody's problems. It was a social thing of its own. If somebody had a problem, all the Grunyons were behind you. Everybody had a real concern for each other, and they still do. Here we are some forty years later, and those things haven't changed at all."

When I took my father to practice several songs before a Christmas show in 2003, I watched the Grunyons' sensitivity to my father's situation in action. They had worked out a buddy system to make sure he didn't get lost on the way to the stage and back. Someone always made sure he was standing in the right place. The person who sang with him in the baritone section stood a bit closer to him than he might have if my father hadn't had Alzheimer's. Someone made sure his tie was tied properly, his shirt was tucked in, and his belt clasp was buckled. When my father had to go to the bathroom, one of the Grunyons would see him heading out in to a hallway and shout something like, "Tagteam" or "Team toilet!" and someone would accompany him there and back.

"Even at his eightieth birthday party just a few months ago," Dick said, "he would ask me what number we were going to do. He'd forget before we'd get to the first note, but as soon as he heard the first note or two, he was right with it. At his birthday, it seemed like he had just a wonderful time. He didn't realize it was his birthday. But the music, for some reason or other, is still there. It just comes out like a natural thing. I can't figure it out."

Dick's eyes filled with tears. "It's tough to see Woody this way, and yet when you're with him, he still has that sparkle in his eye," he said. "When we were learning something new, he would have some difficulty following it at first so I would point it out to him. Otherwise he would get sort of lost, and we never wanted to have him feel lost. And he needed such little prompting. It just took a little bit to remind him of what we were doing next and that kind of thing, and if we were practicing and it was something new to show him where it was and the music—that was no big deal because he would learn it! That kept him in the group for a long time."

I asked Dick whether I'm deluding myself by believing my father knows the words to most of the songs he sings with the Grunyons. Dick says I'm not. "We can't feed him words. I don't know the words to his solos! Tony Alcantra, the director, has sung with him during his solos recently and prompted him when necessary. He had a problem once in a while. Tony just sang some of the words with him."

When I asked Dick, a piano player and singer in the Detroit area, to assess Dad's singing ability after having Alzheimer's for more than a decade, he said, "It's phenomenal! He still knows the songs. He still knows the words. How can that stick with you when virtually nothing else does?"

The words Dick said that day still resound for me: "We never wanted him to feel lost." I thought about how my father's beloved singing group had been like a compass to keep him from being lost for so many years.

I contacted the well-known neurologist and author, Oliver Sacks, who wrote *The Man Who Mistook His Wife for a Hat*, as well as *Awakenings*, which was made into an Oscar-nominated movie, and most recently, *Musicophilia*, as well as many other books that focus on neurological diseases. I told him about my father's musical proclivity and his ability to remember songs, to harmonize, and to remember all the words even though he's had Alzheimer's for more than a decade. In November 2006, my parents and I visited Dr. Sacks at his office in Greenwich Village. He was writing a book about music and brain diseases.

When we walked into Dr. Sacks's office, my father smiled, shook hands with him, and introduced himself. "I'm Woody," he said, as naturally as he would have at a business meeting or a party. I am always struck by how normal my father seems—initially—in social settings. As we sat down, I watched Dr. Sacks assess him. The first thing he did was ask my father what he was carrying in his hands. (I had given him my *New York Times* to carry.) He didn't know what it was. My mother and I were a little taken aback. We both still thought he knew what a newspaper was and how to say the word. Dr. Sacks asked him to read the top of the paper. He couldn't do it. He asked him where he was. He didn't know. But when Dr. Sacks asked my father to sing, so much of the father I remembered came back.

Dad sang along with the Grunyons CD I had brought with us. My mother and I harmonized on several songs with him, too. Dr. Sacks seemed interested and amused. After talking with my father for some time and listening to him sing, Dr. Sacks met with me and then with my mother alone. Dr. Sacks said, "There is so much there that I can just imagine what a great space he took up before he got Alzheimer's." He seemed to understand not only what my father was going through, but also what my mother and I were experiencing as well.

"Your mother is exhausted," he said to me, "and you are clearly suffering from the grief of slowly losing your father." He reinforced my beliefs that my father is an extraordinary man, and has, most likely, been able to remain in this world, our world, and deal with Alzheimer's so gracefully, not only because of the special qualities he possesses including his love and memory of music, but also because of the constant and unfailing love and care given to him by my mother.

Another thing Dr. Sacks said was so poignant for me: "He's a gentleman. All the way down through his Alzheimer's."

Dr. Sacks wrote a beautiful description in his book *Musicophilia* of what music does for my father.

Finding, remembering anew that he *can* sing is profoundly reassuring to Woody, as the exercise of any skill or competence must be—and it can stimulate his feelings, his imagination, his sense of humor and creativity, his sense of identity, as nothing else can. It can enliven him, calm him, focus and engage him. It can give him back himself, and not least, it can charm others, arouse their amazement and admiration—reactions more and more necessary to someone who, in his lucid moments, is painfully aware of his tragic disease, and sometimes says that he feels "broken inside."

Perhaps Woody, though he could not have put it into words, knows that this is the case for him, for in the last year or so, he has taken to whistling. He whistled "Somewhere Over the Rainbow" softly to himself for the entire afternoon we spent together. Whenever he was not actively singing or otherwise engaged, Mary Ellen and Rosemary told me, he now whistles all the while. Not only through his waking hours; he whistles (and sometimes sings) in his sleep—so at least, in this sense, Woody is companioned by music, calls on it, around the clock.

Today, as I was driving with my father, I put the Grunyons CD *Just In Time* in my CD player. "Oh, listen to that!" he said, and then he smiled. It was the first smile I had seen in a while. "Weren't those guys great?" he said. I have been playing the Grunyons CD often as we drive together to go to adult day care, as we go shopping, as we go almost anywhere, and especially if he seems anxious. He seems to know that my jeep will carry certain tunes he likes. He even mouths the words before each song begins because he has memorized the order the songs are in.

When my father sees me punch the button on the CD player in my jeep, he often says, "How did you get this in here?" because the concept of playing music in the car has become foreign to him. But he seems eager to hear it, each time. As we rode in the car together, he said again today, "I don't know where I am." This past summer he added, "Where did I come from?" It's all so strange. I can't imagine what that would feel like. Yet as lost as he feels, when I play music, it seems as if he suddenly feels at home. The muscles in his back seem to relax. He sits back in the seat, calm as a cucumber, and sometimes he says out loud, emphatically, "I love this!"

Once, as we drove in the car and listened to the Keith Jarrett CD *The Melody at Night With You*, one of my favorite songs of all time came on, Jarrett's version of "Don't Ever Leave Me" by Oscar Hammerstein and Jerome Kern. My father heard the first notes and said, "Isn't it so sad?" This is something he often says, but on *this* drive to adult day care, he added something new. He said loudly, "I can feel the notes dying!"

His statement surprised me because he'd been so checked out recently and unable to articulate his feelings. I wondered where this declaration came from. It was the first time I had heard him say this, so I asked him what he meant. He put his hands out, as though he were playing a piano, and he said, "I can just feel the sadness in the notes." "The emotion in the piano playing?" I said, and he said, "Yes." I believe you *can* hear the sadness in Keith Jarrett's piano playing, but I wondered whether my father was superimposing his own emotions onto the music he was hearing. Then I thought, Music is the thing that means the most to him, and now he is telling me that the music is dying.

As Alzheimer's takes him away more, I feel that music is the last link with the world for him. I try to get him to sing every day, desperately wanting to hear him sing every word and every part to as many songs as we can muster. Half a dozen songs a day is good, but at times we sing much more than that, and my mother sings with him, too, as well as my sisters and brothers-in-law and the grandchildren whenever they are with us. We do this as a way to hold on.

I know music and the act of singing calm him. When we are doing a chore together in the house, and he can't remember or figure out certain actions, his comprehension seems to improve if we are singing while we are performing a task. Why would music make tasks easier for him?

I talked with Dr. Connie Tomaino, executive director and cofounder of the Institute for Music and Neurologic Function and senior vice president for Music Therapy Services for the Beth Abraham Family of Health Services in the Bronx. She's been studying the effect of music on people with dementia and Alzheimer's for more than thirty years. She has seen the power of music firsthand.

When she was getting her master's in music therapy at New York University in the mid-'70s, Dr. Tomaino worked at a small nursing home in Brooklyn. She says, "My first assignment was to go to the dementia units, the old, really horrible ones where people had nasal gastric tubes and their hands were put in mitts tied to wheelchairs so they wouldn't pull the tubes out of their noses. Half the people are catatonic, and the other half are agitated and screaming and pulling at their wheelchairs with their mitted hands. I walked onto the unit and I started singing 'Let Me Call You Sweetheart.' The people who had been catatonic opened their eyes and started looking at me, and the people who were agitated calmed down." She says some of the people—many of whom were previously thought to be unable to speak—joined in. "The people who were thought to have no cognitive ability started singing the song with me, actually showing me that they had lots of ability if they used music."

Dr. Tomaino says she started looking for literature about music and the brain and there was basically nothing. Only one or two books addressed the issue at the time, and she couldn't find anything about music helping recall. She says, "I got excited about the potential of music to help people that seemed to be practically removed from reality and unreachable otherwise. That's been my quest, all these years."

When Dr. Tomaino came to Beth Abraham, she asked to work with people who had the most severe dementia. "I started studying and recording case by case how and why music that was familiar to people and had personal importance could affect them so powerfully." Dr. Tomaino is convinced that "familiar music stimulates or activates what's called 'recognition memory.' It's the memories that are very deep, very personal. It activates those centers of the brain that process that information and allows it to get retrieved in a way that's meaningful to that person. There are very few other things that allow that kind of retrieval to take place. Visual processing gets damaged early on. Face recognition is gone. Pictures don't make sense, because the person can't really interpret or make sense of them. But music can transcend those limitations and really reach the memories that are very much alive and accessible to that person. They just need to be turned on. Music has a way of exciting and turning on those mechanisms to make those memories come alive again."

Dr. Tomaino became fascinated with the way music seemed to "light up" the cortex of the brain and help people with diseases such as Alzheimer's improve function on many levels. In 1994 she received one of the first grants given in New York State to study the effects of familiar music on people with dementia.

"I wish everybody knew how powerful music is," says Dr. Tomaino. For people who find out a loved one has Alzheimer's, she recommends that the first thing they should do is to make a CD or write a list of all that person's favorite songs and begin playing and singing the songs with the person as often as possible. "When you do it early on in the disease process, you're basically reinforcing those memories, so at the end stages, when it seems like nothing else is possible, those songs will still have meaning. It's a way for families to share moments together." She says that by playing or singing familiar songs over and over again, "You have a way of improving connections and exciting residual parts of the brain that can be called back into action."

Dr. Tomaino says for the caregiver, "Music allows connections to remain. It allows people to be with each other in a way they couldn't be if music weren't present. The person is never gone, it's just that who that individual is, is somehow trapped in this body that has lost so much function. But there is part of them that is very much there and able to be connected to. In those moments of sharing music, couples, families, kids—they have a way of maintaining contact in a meaningful, powerful way that wouldn't be possible otherwise."

"A growing body of research suggests that music, like art, pets, and other creative forms of therapy, can stir emotions and memories, enhance enjoyment and self-esteem, and enrich the lives of people with dementia. Relaxation with the type of music that calms you down is very beneficial," says Dr. Adarsh Kumar, a music therapy researcher at the University of Miami School of Medicine in Florida. "To promote a sense of calm and well-being, you can listen to your favorite soothing music when you eat, before you sleep, and when you want to relax. Like meditation and yoga, it can help us maintain our hormonal balance, even during periods of stress or disease."

Dr. Kumar and her fellow researchers found that music provided lasting benefits to elderly men with Alzheimer's disease. The men were provided with music therapy for thirty to forty minutes a day, five days a week, for a month. For weeks after joining the musical program, the men showed less disruptive behavior, slept better, and became generally more active and cooperative.

Dr. Kumar also found that "while people with Alzheimer's may lose the ability to speak or recognize loved ones as the disease takes its inexorable downward decline, many retain the ability to remember songs from long-ago childhoods. Singing a round of 'Rock-a-Bye Baby' may help to ease agitation, for example, during difficult times of the day, such as when the sun goes down or when moving from one room to another. Humming a few bars of 'Home on the Range' may be comforting and reassuring to a person with Alzheimer's disease, who may not even recognize the loved one standing in front of them."

Dianne Tow is a music therapist at Sherrill House in Boston, a nonprofit skilled nursing home. The Alzheimer's and dementia special care program is designed around a therapeutic schedule that provides activities for residents of different cognitive levels twelve hours a day, seven days a week. Dianne says music opens up portals to memory, love, and language for people with Alzheimer's. "It focuses on something that has meaning and purpose rather than distracting them. And it's amazing how music can enhance a person's mood. I've also seen physiological changes. People who are wanderers can even work themselves into a sweat from wandering back and forth. They're looking for something, but they don't know what it is. Music can serve to focus their attention. Music can help them stop, slow down, and even sit down. You can even see their breathing patterns change with music. You can see them calm down physically."

I asked Dianne if she has seen long-term benefits of music therapy for Alzheimer's patients. "I wish I could say that I see a lot of long-lasting effects, but so much of Alzheimer's disease and the tragedy of it is that all there are, are moments. What I have seen is that for the people who are incredibly agitated, music can bring them to another place. They are not agitated anymore. They are more calm, and that calm will last after the music therapy session is over. I have noticed also long-lasting effects in Alzheimer's patients who were previously unengaged."

Christmas 2006. My mother said that in the middle of the night, while my father was still in a deep sleep, he had shouted "Merry Christmas" in a cheerful tone and then sang the first verse of "Jingle Bells" with all the words and his baritone part intact, all the way through. Then he started snoring again. If that's not evidence of the power of music, I don't know what is.

Music and the sphere of comfort it creates seem to envelop the heart and soul and brain of my father and make Alzheimer's go away for just a little while. It provides a way for him to tell us that he is still inside, even when he's in a deep sleep. He can't read a newspaper. He can't read a book. But when words are placed along a music staff, he can read the lyrics to a song. Music opens a pathway into my father's brain.

When my little sister, Libby, was about six years old and my father determined that she was able to sing and read notes as well as (or maybe better than) the rest of us, he decided that we, as a family, should try to sing a cappella songs together. He had some sort of Von Trapp Family fantasy, and we obliged.

We sat down at the piano and tried it, and when we harmonized together for the first time, I saw my father's face light up. I remember that moment around the piano. He seemed to have this puffed-up sense of pride. When we hit a chord properly and our voices blended and it made the chord "ring," he would stop for a moment, raise his finger in the air, and smile. We started rehearsing songs together. You could often find the five of us gathered around the piano. It's the place where we worked out not only songs, but also many family dynamics. We hammered out conflicts, picked on each other, bickered, and begged forgiveness. We didn't deal with conflict and family dynamics so well in our normal lives, but we learned to work things through as we rehearsed around the piano. Music provided a way for us to communicate with each other.

We have a recording of our family singing the song from the musical *Oliver*, "Where Is Love," when Libby was very young. Her voice is lovely, innocent, and strong, like my father's voice on the record he made when he was almost the same age. Whenever he hears the recording, my father says something like, "Is that someone I know?" I say, "That's our whole family, Dad, and Libby, your youngest daughter, is singing the solo!" At that point he usually says, "I'm so proud!"

I ended up singing professionally with a jazz band for a time. My father and my mother came to see me sing whenever I performed near their home outside Detroit. I'm not sure my father liked the selection of songs I sang (although I sang a lot of jazz standards, what was called funk was popular at the time), but I believe he was proud I had followed the dream of singing professionally, even if my pitch wasn't as perfect as it should have been and the songs might not have been the ones he would have chosen to sing. I made several recordings, and even though all the songs weren't to his liking, he sent the records to many people he knew.

As my father's Alzheimer's progresses beyond a decade, music is the only thing he seems to truly hang on to. It continues to be what links us together, too. It is the way we "talk" with my father, I suppose, as the words fall away.

About ten years into my father's disease, music became a part of my father and my mother's life in a new way. He started whistling—soft little whistles at first, throughout the day, and just once in a while. Then he started whistling for long periods of time. His lips began pursing together between bites of cereal at the breakfast table and during dinner. At the beginning, it was just when there was nothing else going on. But now he whistles all day long, from the moment he wakes up until he goes to sleep. My mother announced the other day that she had timed it and it worked out to approximately ten hours of whistling each day. She wondered whether it might actually be damaging his lips and cheeks to whistle this much.

Most of the time, he seems to know that he shouldn't whistle when we're out in public. We have learned how to urge him to stop whistling during movies and most performances and lectures by nudging him or putting a finger against our lips. He always obliges. Until he forgets. We remind him again. He quits. Then he starts again. When all else fails, there are Gummi Bears, Mentos, Cinnamon Bears, and Jujyfruits.

When we go out to restaurants, we try to keep him from whistling when he isn't chewing his food, but it is becoming impossible. The only time he seems to stop whistling these days is while he's eating or sleeping. Until recently.

The other morning (November 15, 2006—I wrote it in my journal), my mother emerged from the bedroom she shares with my father looking a bit bedraggled and as though she hadn't slept much. "It finally happened!" she proclaimed. "I knew it was just a matter of time. Your father has started to whistle in his sleep!" Fortunately, my mother says it is only for short periods of time, and—so far, anyway—he usually whistles softly.

We have a rule in our family: Since Dad started his trademark nonstop whistling, none of the rest of us are allowed to whistle. Ever. So the other day when my father was at adult day care and my mother started whistling in the house, I yelled loudly, "Stop!"

Sometimes, though, we can't help it. We whistle anyway. What's worse is that when I am finally alone, I sometimes find myself whistling just the way my father does. I seem to have inherited his sort of windy tone. And it is true: sometimes I start whistling the incessant tune he keeps whistling over and over again that none of us can positively identify: "ta-dah-dah-dah-dah-dah dah-DAH!" Then up a third: "tah-dah-dah-dah-dah-dah-dah-dah dah-DAH!"

It is possible that my father's incessant whistling and his love of music have actually helped to slow the progression of Alzheimer's and have helped relieve some of the symptoms. It is yet another way my father has instinctively done his best to keep himself as healthy as possible along this slow decline toward the final result of Alzheimer's.

One day my father and I were driving around in the car listening to a CD of the Grunyons. Suddenly, he turned to me and said, "Are those guys still alive?" I said, "Yes. Except for one." On April 14, 2006, one of the Grunyons, Charlie Parcells, had died at age eighty-six.

"Oh," he said. He was quiet for a little while. He didn't even whistle for a time. I could tell he was thinking about something. Then a very bizarre thing happened. My father said, "That's what I want." I said, "What?" and he said, "That's how I want to die." I said, "What way, Dad? Singing?" He said, "Sort of." I said, "What do you mean, then, Dad?" hoping that he might stay lucid with me through this thread of thought. He said, "With those guys." I said, "Do you mean you want to die singing with the Grunyons?" He said with a very confident tone, "Yes!" and then he smiled. He started whistling again then, a sweet and clear sound.

Chapter Nine

The Caregivers

W HEN YOU ARE HELPING TO CARE FOR someone who has Alzheimer's, some days seem longer than others. One day I spent an inordinate amount of time trying to get my father ready to go out the door. Usually, my mother does the majority of the morning routine of helping him to shower, shave, and take his pills. But on this particular morning, she had an early appointment, and I had promised her she could go ahead without waking up Dad and getting him ready. I told her I would get him out of bed and out the door, and that I knew I could do it on my own.

My job was preparing him to go to adult day care. One of us takes him there two or three times a week. After I drop him off, usually at about 10:30 or 11 a.m., I write for several hours, go to the gym, then pick him up at 3 p.m. Afterward, Dad and I often spend several hours together so my mother can have more time alone. We go grocery shopping, play tennis, get a milkshake, or do various errands. Then we drive around in my jeep singing and listening to CDs.

I thought it sounded easy enough to add the "Dad prep" part to my day, and to do this by myself. I'd pull it off with no problem!

For some reason, the morning I was taking care of him without my mother's help, even the sight of his shoes didn't compute.

"Here, Dad," I shouted too loudly by the side of his bed as I tried to make him see his shoes and socks and move faster so I could get him to adult day care on time. It seemed to take a half hour just to tie his shoelaces. He was groggier than usual. I had to hold up the shaver and make motions across my own face to remind him what shaving was. I sprayed the shaving cream in his hand, but he forgot what it was and rinsed it off in the sink like soap. I had to spray a second application on his hand and we tried it again. I was exasperated. Finally, when he sat down to breakfast, he simply would not put his spoon in the cereal bowl. He just stared across the breakfast table for some time. I kept urging him to begin his breakfast, but he wouldn't move. Finally, I said rudely, "Eat, Dad! We're late!"

First, he stirred the cereal and milk around and around until I thought I might scream. Then he clinked his spoon against the edge of the bowl repeatedly, for no particular reason. Then he slowly, slowly took a bite of his Frosted Mini-Wheats.

Somehow (after what seemed like an hour but was probably more like thirty minutes) we made it back to his bathroom. I combed his hair and tamped down the cowlick on the back of his head with some hair gel. I put toothpaste on his toothbrush and mimicked brushing my own teeth before I handed the toothbrush to him. I handed him his pills.

"What are these for?" he said in a shocked voice, as he says every single morning and every single night. But as he does every time, he gulped them down with the glass of water I handed to him. I made sure he wiped his nose. I stuffed his pockets with Kleenex. I even put aftershave under his ears and on his face and wrists because the people at adult day care have a great affection for him and the women, in particular, often hug him (and he likes to hug them back). Like my mother, I always feel better if I know he smells really good when he heads out the door.

I finally got him to the closet in the foyer. Snow was coming down in big, fat flakes, and I wanted to make sure he'd be warm. I sifted through the hangers to find his long khaki-colored winter coat. (It took a while because Dad had apparently hung it inside out and then it had fallen off the hanger and was crumpled in the bottom of the closet.) I wrapped his black wool scarf around his neck. I moved his hands into soft mittens (for me, gloves take too long and are often too difficult for him to figure out anymore).

He was finally ready to go. "Where are we going?" he said for the hundredth time that morning. "Adult day care, Dad, remember? Judy and Lisa and all your friends. They'll all be there. And remember you sing and you make crafts?"

Why do I ask him questions I know he can't answer each morning? I wonder this often. Maybe it's delusional thinking coupled with complete denial that makes me believe that one morning he'll be able to remember and answer correctly. As usual, when I ask him questions like this, he nods and pretends he remembers. "Oh yes!" he says. Then one minute later he says, "Where are we going?" again. We talked like this as he finished buttoning up his coat.

He was ready to go. I went to the foyer to get my purse and keys. And then I realized I was still wearing my pajamas! I hadn't even brushed my hair since I woke up, and I hadn't even brushed my teeth!

Other caregivers tell me that the same kinds of things have happened to them countless times. Some caregivers say it's even worse than almost—or even actually—wearing your pajamas to a public place. They forget their own needs completely, physical as well as emotional.

Neglect. Not of the person you're taking care of. Of yourself. Don't let anyone tell you otherwise—taking care of an Alzheimer's patient can make you crazy. At times I think I'm going over the edge. I might as well go into an institution *with* him! And I might still be wearing my pajamas, with unkempt hair, as they take me away. I know Mom has felt this way at times over the years, and now I do, too.

Every time I do something such as get my father ready to head out the door, spend an entire day with him, or even spend a weekend alone with him without my mother's help (I have only done that a few times), I think, How has my mother done this alone all these years? Somehow, she not only gets Dad ready each morning, but she also emerges from their home perfectly coiffed, with a lovely outfit, including earrings (often with necklaces and bracelets that match), and she even puts on makeup. Somehow, she even incorporates a curling iron into their morning routine.

I think about it every day: How does she do it? How do caregivers—in particular, spouses—take care of their Alzheimer's-afflicted loved ones on their own and even look beautiful doing it? Most of all, how do they keep from flipping out? Some of them don't. Many decline along with the person living with Alzheimer's. If their mental health doesn't deteriorate, often their bodies do.

In a national study released in September 2006 by the Evercare Study of Caregivers in collaboration with the National Alliance for Caregiving, stress emerged as the symptom that stands out most. The caregivers surveyed reported a downward spiral of health as a result of giving care. Their overall health status was reported as fair to poor. The most common aspects of their health that had worsened as a result of caregiving were as follows: energy and sleep (87 percent), stress and/or panic attacks (70 percent), pain, aching (60 percent), depression (52 percent), headaches (41 percent), and weight gain/loss (38 percent). Caregivers noted that stress was the most pervasive health problem in their lives. They said they worry constantly about their care-recipients' well-being and whether more can be done to help them.

Each day of caring for someone with Alzheimer's is a challenge. Each day is like hiking up a big mountain and never, ever getting to the top. When you get near the top of the mountain, you fall back down and have to start over again. You feel like a failure often. Instead of gains and results, such as a mother or a teacher might experience with a child, with an Alzheimer's patient all you have are losses. This often results in a decline in self-esteem.

How do you take care of yourself and the Alzheimer's patient, too? It is close to impossible. To make sure you don't accidentally wear your pajamas to the store, however, my mother says it is necessary to have a routine.

"Here's how I do it," she says. "I get up and lay out the things he's going to need for shaving in the bathroom. (I try to get up before he wakes up so I can do this.) I put the clean underwear in the bathroom, I lay out his clothes, and I put his socks on top of his shoes." (She does this, of course, because if she didn't place the clothes in the proper progression in the proper places, they might wind up on the wrong part of his anatomy. Or he might pull his underwear up over his pants.)

"If he's going to take a shower, I get the temperature right on the water, and I put his towel out so he'll know which one is his. I reach in and put the shampoo on his head while he's in the shower, and I scrub and encourage him to scrub his own hair. If you don't do this, he won't shampoo. After he puts his undershorts on, I go on and help put the shaving cream on his face. But he can shave himself.

"So now he's shaved and you have to supervise him as he gets dressed. For instance, this morning I wasn't watching, and he had his shorts on backwards. He said, 'Are they upside down or wrong side out?' I couldn't get him to understand what was wrong.

"So then he's dressed. And he says, 'Shall I get the newspaper?' and I say, 'Yes.' He says, 'Which one is it?' or 'Where is it?'"

I have watched my mother and father perform this routine on many mornings since I came home. He stands in the doorway and points to the end of the driveway as he asks her questions. Then he goes out to the end of the driveway and gets the paper. Sometimes he brings the mail back, too. Somehow, he always makes his way back to the front door. The minute he gets inside, he wants to know if he can turn on "the radio" (the TV).

My mother says, "During this time, I'm trying to get dressed. I try to take a quick shower while he's going out to get the newspaper. If the opportunity comes up, I'll do as much as I can to get myself ready. Meantime, I'm heating up my curling iron and washing my face."

If my mother isn't waiting for him in the kitchen with breakfast prepared, often he will come back to the bedroom because he doesn't know what to do when he's alone. Or he stands in the center of the living room or in the kitchen. I hear him sometimes when I'm upstairs in my bedroom, saying, "What should I be doing?" to no one in particular. Or he'll shout, "Can I do something?" It must feel so strange to feel lost all the time in your own home. What a frightening prospect—like a constant scary funhouse or one of those crooked houses where the dimensions are purposefully altered like the ones at Knott's Berry Farm.

When I first came home, my mother and I had Dad help us a lot in the kitchen, but we don't do it much anymore. It's too difficult. My mother says, "He always wants to help, but he doesn't know how anymore. Sometimes I let him pour the juice or some simple part of getting breakfast ready. Sometimes I put some makeup on and then run back and do some more. We always have breakfast together. He always asks if he can put on 'the radio.' I try not to do that in the morning. I try to read the paper to him, but he can't visualize what I'm reading to him anymore."

If he does help out, there's often evidence left behind. Juice is spilled on the floor. Pieces of fruit wind up in unusual places. (He likes to hang things lately. Recently he hung a banana peel over the kitchen faucet in a decorative fashion.) Frosted Mini-Wheats wind up ground into the rug.

It wouldn't matter so much if we had time to clean up the mess after he helps us with chores. But in the morning, if there's a schedule to keep, we wouldn't be able to get him to adult day care in time. So we have stopped including him in morning chores; it's just too difficult and time consuming.

When I came home two years ago, Dad asked questions about how the day was going to go. He repeated things over and over. Now he doesn't say much of anything, except, from time to time, "When did I get sick?" or, "How long have I been here?" He whistles up until he puts the spoon filled with cereal to his mouth. He whistles again the minute he has swallowed. Sometimes the crunching followed by whistling is as depressing as all get-out. So sometimes we play music—Frank Sinatra or a cappella music or a CD of the Grunyons. When the music begins, his shoulders relax. Sometimes he begins to smile and says, "Isn't that wonderful?" Music in the morning always helps.

On the days we take him to adult day care, my mother gets the two of them out the door with much more grace than I can muster. I asked my mother what she does to take care of her own mental health. She said, "I see a therapist, and I think it's important to do if you're going through this. The problem is that you lose yourself. It's all about him. You no longer really know what you want or what you'd like to do. You just think in terms of what he'd like to do. And he doesn't know what he wants to do either, for different reasons."

I asked her why she doesn't seem to see very many people socially anymore. "We see a few people, but not very often," she explained. "Sometimes we'll see somebody for dinner or go to a movie. It's harder to see people these days because he doesn't remember them. And I think it's awkward for other people, too, and not many people call anymore. I think it's because this disease makes them uncomfortable."

My mother says she doesn't blame them, either. "I think people are afraid. They don't know what he might do or what their responsibility is. They don't know where he is in the progression. I think they're uneasy about what they can say and how to handle it. However, other people are very nurturing. There's a couple we're close to, and they're very nice about inviting us. At the dinner table, our friend will get up and pull a chair next to Woody and try to have a conversation. He'll talk to him. But it's hard when you don't get much in the way of a response."

I mentioned to my mother that it seems she doesn't even try to go out in the evening anymore. "Going out at night is just too difficult most of the time," she said. "He wants to go to sleep at 8 or 9 o'clock. Plus I'm exhausted at the end of the day."

"Going to see Meredith [her therapist] keeps me centered," she said. "She makes me think about myself and what I want and what I need and try to focus on what I can do for myself." My mother says one of Meredith's most important roles is that of urging her to think about her *own* future, separate from my father. She says Meredith asks her things like, "What are my plans immediately? Am I going to see people? Have lunch? Go to choir rehearsal? Then there's the long range. When does it become too difficult? When do I have to move out of this house to save my own life? She helps me plan for the next phase of my life. She helps me to think about it."

My mother says that since I came home I have also provided a sounding board for her. "Time alone with you, so we can talk about what's going on—that helps." Since I came home, I have watched the ways my mother and I respond to my father's needs and the way we try to keep him occupied, happy, and comfortable. It is often at the cost of our own happiness and comfort, because he's the sick one. He's the one who needs our help. This makes sense. It's what my mother is used to. But it is all new territory for me.

I have sudden outbursts of anger or sadness. I suddenly need to get away, go on a walk, exercise, or have time alone. I don't see my mother explode like this. She sits calmly on the couch next to my dad while he whistles and watches CNN. She incorporates paper-work, folding laundry, paying bills, mending, or other activities into his caregiving.

My mother is stronger than I am. I have to get away periodically to save my sanity. I ask her what keeps her from going off the deep end. "Quiet time at night, reading, watching TV," she says. "But it's often the quiet time alone that restores me the most. I try to read the paper at night because I can't read it during the day."

In the book *Alzheimer's: A Caregiver's Guide and Sourcebook*, Howard Gruetzner has created what he calls the Caregiver's Bill of Rights. The first right he lists is this: "The right to make decisions on be-half of loved ones and ourselves that support what is best for both of us." The second right is "The right to have time and activities for ourselves without guilt, fear or criticism." The second right causes the most problems for almost every caregiver I've talked with. It is also what could stand between happiness and sadness, health and sickness, for so many caregivers.

One evening, my mother discussed why helping to take care of an Alzheimer's patient is so emotionally draining and potentially crazy-making, and why it's so difficult to do the things you need to do to keep you happy when you are taking care of someone who is living with Alzheimer's. She said, "It's because you can't fix it. You can't reach him. You're grieving all the time. The man you were married to and loved is really no longer there. And yet he is."

I talked with Carol Levine, director of the Families and Health Care Project at the United Hospital Fund in New York City and co-editor of the books *The Cultures of Caregiving* and *Always on Call: When Illness Turns Families Into Caregivers*. For seventeen years, she took care of her husband, who had suffered brain damage in an accident and was severely disabled. She says respite care would have helped her mental health during that period of time: "It would be nice if there were places that would take people short term, if, God for-bid, I wanted to go away for a week or two weeks, if there would have been a place that could have handled his care during that period of time that I would feel confident about. But that didn't exist."

Levine said many caregivers refuse to admit that the person they're taking care of isn't managing well at home anymore. Often, the caregiver's own health crisis prompts placement in a nursing home. One of the reasons caregivers' mental and physical health become precarious is that no particular organization is checking in on their state of mind and body. According to Levine, "The health care system is not doing enough for the caregiver."

During the almost two decades that Levine took care of her husband at home, what she needed most was someone to just talk with and vent to on a regular basis, someone to ask for help when she needed it. Instead, she felt alone and isolated and often asked, "Who can I call to talk with when I have problems managing my husband's situation? There was absolutely no one in the system who cared about me, no one on my side who would be my advocate and my husband's advocate, to work *with* me so I'd feel there was some backup and support."

Levine explained: "We have to be able to accept when something is not going right, and to really talk about it. It doesn't mean the person is going into a nursing home the next day, but if you don't talk about it, you pretend it doesn't exist. It gets worse and worse, and then there's a crisis like a fall and a terrible cascade of medical problems. It's a bad situation. People don't want to talk about it. I don't know how you get people to talk about it. Primary care doctors could do better and be more alert and could recognize when the family is struggling with something."

While she was taking care of her husband, Levine said, "I didn't appreciate what a toll this was taking on me because *he* was the one with the terrible problem. I found myself avoiding doctors and avoiding finding out anything that was really wrong with me because I was so afraid of having to make a choice between caregiving and taking care of myself. I avoided having hip replacements for a year and a half because I felt I couldn't do it. I wound up in terrible, excruciating, unbearable pain. There was no reason for that. I should have been able to say, I can't do this. I didn't ask for help when I should have. I didn't make mistakes for *him*, but I did for me. I thought I was able to do everything. The total way I organized my life was around his needs, not mine."

Seeing a therapist was helpful for Levine. "It's important to have someone to talk with who will keep you centered." I asked her about the residual effects of taking care of her husband for seventeen years. "I feel unalterably changed," she told me. "I don't feel like much of it has been good. In some ways, I feel satisfied that I did the right thing and that I did the best I could in every way. I don't feel any regrets about what I did, but I feel very much that I gave a huge amount of my life and got very little in return. And that's hard because he couldn't give it.

"I have this unbelievable sadness about all of this," Levine said, "and it never goes away. The sadness was there when he was alive, and the sadness is still there now that he's gone. I miss just walking into his room and making sure he's okay, but at the same time now if somebody says, 'Do you want to go out to dinner?' I can say 'Sure,' but I have to think about it for a minute. I can't tell you how hard it is for me to be a normal person again. I am not one of the caregivers who says, 'It's so rewarding and I loved it and I would do it again.' But I don't see an alternative or what else I could have done."

Susan Strecker Richard, editor-in-chief of *Caring Today* magazine, says that one of the reasons caregivers put their mental and physical health at risk is simply because they feel so alone. That sense of isolation is one of the most common themes among her readers. Strecker Richard says *Caring Today* was started in 2004 to respond to the growing needs of family caregivers who were entering into new and changing roles with little or no guidance. The magazine stepped in to fill a big void and offer support, encouragement, facts, and resources to help people be the best caregivers they can be for their loved ones. *Caring Today* also emphasizes taking care of oneself, understanding how to get help and tame stress, avoiding burnout, eating well, and exercising daily—all for the sake of mental and physical well-being.

Strecker Richard says, "Many caregivers simply feel they have nowhere to turn. They suffer from the emotions and the stress, in addition to the logistics. In addition to the doctor's appointments and all the physical requirements of caregivers, there's so much worry. The caregiver is being pulled in so many directions and doesn't know where to turn. So many people aren't good at asking for help, and there is so much guilt."

Guilt, stress, burnout, physical and emotional health problems caused by neglect—these are just a few of the symptoms caregivers face. Yet even with all these potential problems, I have the distinct feeling that my mother will never get to the point that she might walk out the door with her pajamas on.

Chapter Ten

The Rituals of Denial

I AM BEGINNING TO UNDERSTAND THAT CAREGIVERS hang on very tightly to the things that remind them of the world they lived in before the disease arrived. I am convinced it is why my mother needs the house clean and orderly even more than she used to. I believe she does this to impose order on her own physical existence. Or maybe it's a way to impose control on the disease and on my father, and to remember the way life was before my father got Alzheimer's.

She scrubs the kitchen sink clean almost every morning (perhaps this is common practice for many people, but it is a foreign act to someone like me). The other day, as I watched her, I thought, Maybe she thinks by bleaching and scrubbing the sink, she can scrub the plaque out of my father's brain. There is a new fervor to her cleanliness and orderliness since my father's Alzheimer's hit, and she admits it.

Certain patterns of daily life are a comfort to my mother. She says one daily routine that is extremely important to her is sleeping together at night. She says, "Then it's all as it was before he had Alzheimer's and we can hold each other and I can put my arm around him and my head goes on his chest the way it always used to before he got sick. It's a comfort to me, and I believe it's a comfort to him, too. When I get in bed at the end of a long day, he's often already asleep and I snuggle up and he raises his arm the way he used to. I feel a sense of peace and love."

She also admits that it's a delusion, of sorts. When he's asleep, there are no signs of his disease. She can pretend that he's the man she married, instead of the man he is now—the man with Alzheimer's.

My mother also enjoys the ritual of having a glass of wine while watching the news with my father at night. The two of them can be found in the family room almost every weeknight at 6 p.m., my mother sitting on the large couch, my father in his reclining chair, watching *The NewsHour with Jim Lehrer* on public television. Since I came home, I have joined them in this ritual.

It isn't clear whether my father understands much of the news anymore. When there are stories about the Iraq War, he says "Why? Why?" repeatedly. A story about a murder upsets him terribly. "What a mess!" he says sometimes. I wonder often whether it might be too upsetting for him to watch the latest events broadcast in harsh detail from across the globe. Joanne Koenig Coste, who wrote the book *Learning to Speak Alzheimer's*, advises against having late-stage Alzheimer's patients watch the news. She says many patients think what's happening on the TV screen is actually happening inside their homes. She says the TV can breed fear and anxiety in people living with Alzheimer's. Yet my father seems to derive comfort from the drone of the television, especially programs he's watched for several decades.

Watching the news each night keeps a routine from my mother and father's former life, and my dad seems to look forward to this time as well. An alarm seems to go off in his brain and body each evening. As the time for the news draws near, he starts searching for "the radio" and asking for "something to drink." Water or a Coke or chocolate milk won't do. Having a glass of wine (or grape juice that looks and tastes like wine) seems to make him feel proud, as though he's in a special club with the rest of us. After the wine is poured, he always toasts. Sometimes he toasts dozens of times, because he doesn't remember toasting even though it may have happened just a minute ago. He wants anyone who's in the house to sit down next to him and watch the news and drink wine and respond to his many toasts by clinking their glasses against his. "Why don't you come here and sit with me?" he often says to us. Performing this nightly ritual is, I believe, a way to communicate for him. It's as strong a ritual as singing is. It's a way to say, I can be the same as you.

We usually sit down to dinner at 7:30 or 8 p.m. At around 9 p.m., another alarm seems to go off in my father's brain to tell him it's time to go to bed. Either Mom or I give him his pills and put out his toothpaste and toothbrush. He always says, "What pills? Why do I need pills?" Then he obediently gulps them down. We help him brush his teeth. He turns down the bedspread and fluffs the pillows, he takes off his shoes and his shirt and his pants, and slides into bed. He's asleep (and sometimes snoring, whistling, talking, or even singing in his dreams) in moments.

Each morning, as my father's disease progresses, he seems more and more lost, and there are fewer daily routines to hang on to. As he becomes more confused, the rituals he is able to perform mean even more to all of us.

My mother wants to keep as many rituals and routines going as we possibly can, no matter how much might be required of her (and of him). So even though we have to show him where the newspaper box is and describe it in detail every morning, she has my father walk to the end of the lane to bring the newspaper back to the house every morning. He has done this for fifty-three years at this house along this driveway. I believe he instinctively knows it's important to perform tasks like this, to prove he can still do them. I have come to believe that he knows he should do these things not just for him, but for my mother, to prove there is still a remnant of the Woody she once knew inside.

So each morning he brings the newspaper back triumphantly and slaps it on the breakfast table. I watch him look around to see if my mother has noticed that he has accomplished this task. It doesn't matter that sometimes he walks out the front door and then walks back inside several times to ask her what he was going out for, and that she has to point to the yellow box and describe it and the newspaper ("the thing rolled up inside; pull it out and bring it inside the house") over and over again. Sometimes she sends him out to the mailbox and he can't seem to find it or has difficulty opening it. Stamped outgoing mail that we thought he was putting in the mailbox in the morning often piles up in the newspaper box instead.

Another ritual that is important for my mother, though difficult, is going to church on Sunday mornings. Again, I ask the question: Is she doing this for herself or for him? Does he get enjoyment out of all this? Does it make sense to roust him from bed early Sunday morning to stand in the pews surrounded by people whose names he can't remember? Yet I know church has always held an important place in his life. It must do him good to be greeted so warmly, to be hugged by so many, to feel the love surround him, and to sing songs he knows so well.

By going to church every Sunday morning, my mother can pretend that my father is the way he was before. She is going through the motions of life as it used to be, participating in the delusion of normality. We do it every day, and every day it seems to be more difficult for my father and more exhausting for my mother. Many people don't realize the toll these delusions and trying to live what resembles a normal life with a person who has Alzheimer's take until it's too late.

At times I think my mother and I have perpetuated the fantasy that my father can live normally for so long that we can't stop doing it, even though he no longer really has the skills to perform some of these tasks. Now we're trapped in the delusion.

The thing about being a caregiver for someone with Alzheimer's is that you don't realize the pervasiveness of the pain until one day you have somehow allowed yourself to sit alone at a café and you feel differently about yourself and the whole world because he isn't with you. The constant repeated questions and the whistling have stopped, and you suddenly feel free in a way you haven't felt for months, or in my mother's case, for years. I am convinced it is harder for my mother and perhaps any spouse who is the main caregiver to do the things she needs to do to keep sane than it is for someone like me.

Because I lived alone for so long, I knew there were things I needed to do to survive my stressful job. They are considered luxuries, even more so now that I have come home to live in a small town in Michigan. I have always thought of these this way: isn't it worth paying sixty bucks for a massage now rather than hundreds or maybe thousands of dollars for years of therapy and antidepressants and lingering neck and back pain that could turn into chronic problems later on? I swear, some of the routines that single career women like me practice, that many people consider opulent luxuries, are actually worthwhile investments in one's mental health and can be very helpful to caregivers. Even small things such as a weekly manicure and pedicure can help immensely.

The activity that helps my state of mind, and would help many caregivers, is any kind of exercise, whenever I can find the time. Biking is a wonderful escape. You get away from the house and you see vistas. You get the feeling of riding away to a new location. You can get winded in a fast-pedaling, sweaty workout, or you can take a leisurely ride.

In winter, cross-country skiing out the back door for just twenty minutes can put me in a much better mood and improve my entire day. Bird-watching in any season is a welcome diversion. Just taking a walk alone, completely alone, is key, even if for just fifteen minutes. You'll return to the person you're taking care of with a new perspective if you just let yourself get away for a little while.

In the summer, I windsurf, waterski, kayak, or sail whenever I have time. Sometimes I put my father in the kayak or the sailboat, too. Even though it's difficult getting him ready to go, I am almost always glad I brought him.

But, doing activities alone is imperative to the survival of a caregiver. You could just stroll down a street or go to a museum, even if you can only go for a half hour. Read a book or a newspaper alone in a library or in a café, or just sit quietly in a coffee shop. But you also need to "debrief." You need a person to vent with, to share the pain. My mother and I help each other by talking at night after my father has gone to bed. My girlfriends (most of them live far away) and my two sisters help me get through difficult times, too. Long late-night phone calls are an elixir for me.

No matter how much pampering you do, however, no matter how much walking or biking or working out in a gym, sometimes the best thing in the whole wide world is just to be alone and do nothing at all. In warm weather, simply go sit on a bench in a park or under a tree somewhere. Just breathe the air. If you can't get away, though, close a door. Make a small place for yourself in your home that is all your own. If you are the primary caregiver and you can't leave, let yourself have alone time late at night after the person you are taking care of is asleep.

In a book called *Gentlecare: Changing the Experience of Alzheimer's Disease in a Positive Way*, author Moyra Jones explains the dangerous place caregivers can put themselves in:

> Family caregivers are greatly at risk for clinical depression and rarely seek or receive treatment for this serious illness. Some research suggests that 40 to 60 percent of caregivers are clinically depressed. Depression not only makes caregiving intolerable for the person offering care, but it dramatically

affects the functioning of the person with dementia. People with dementia are acutely aware of the feelings this disease engenders among others in the environment, and are unable to find respite from that oppressive knowledge and burden.

Overriding every other feeling, however, is the smoldering pain of grief. The grief that follows physical death is understood and accepted by our society. But grief associated with chronic illness is frequently ignored or misunderstood. Sometimes family caregivers will say, 'I can't understand why I act the way I do; or why do I seem to be crying all the time; or why do I get so mad at him?' Rarely do they identify these emotional outbursts as emanating from prolonged, overwhelming grief.

Mourning someone who has not physically died, and who therefore falls outside the universally recognized rituals of mourning, places caregivers in an odd position: no flowers are sent; no sympathy cards arrive in the mail; no sympathy phone calls are received. And, in fact, no one may call at all.

And yet death surrounds the caregiver. With dementia, unlike physical illness, the sick person is physically healthy for much of the duration of the disease process. What is grieved by the family is the death of the personality—the loss of the essential human being.

So the grief of dementia is clandestine: grief is hidden, repressed or changed to a more socially acceptable emotion like guilt. If caregivers admit to feeling bereaved, they are often reminded that the person with dementia is still alive. It is easier and more socially acceptable to be guilty than to grieve when you have lost a loved one to Alzheimer's disease.

According to Jones, therapy of some sort can be lifesaving for the caregiver. "Family members who acknowledge their grief and receive support and therapy talk about a weight being lifted from their lives. They speak of renewed energy and a greater understanding of the actions of the sick person.

"Help with anticipatory grieving is rarely discussed with families, nor is it readily available. Without such help, families continue down the slippery slope into a state of apathy. This classic feeling of helplessness is the inevitable outcome of chronic fatigue, sorrow, and isolation."

Jones's words hit home. Chronic fatigue. Sorrow. Isolation. These three words described how I believe my mother was feeling before I came home. Jones says there is a price to pay for getting to this stage of grief without a support system in place: "Lack of respite is the Achilles' heel of the family caregiver. Abuse occurs, it seems to me, in one of two ways: either the family caregiver sacrifices his or her health in an attempt to meet the needs of the person with dementia; or the caregiver goes beyond the breaking point and physically or psychologically abuses the person with dementia. Both types of abuse are systemic and pervasive in dementia care. Frequently the caregiver is not aware of what is happening."

The family caregiver "sacrifices his or her health in an attempt to meet the needs of the person with dementia." That's what I believe was happening to my mother before I came home. It is one of the many reasons I returned. It is still happening to some degree right now, but I believe it has lessened since I've been here. I try to help get my mother out the door to do things on her own. I try to remind her of things she finds enjoyable and encourage her to do them.

I believe that having two people (and, if possible, two family members) take care of someone like my father can make all the difference in the world. I can not only help with taking care of my father, but also acknowledge the hell my mother has been going through. I can also keep an eye on her health. Because we are family, we can vent with each other, share our feelings, and check up on each other's well-being.

This past Valentine's Day (2007) the three of us went to a French restaurant. We ate delicious food, and the owners of the restaurant brought us fresh roses. My mother and I discussed our trip to Paris long ago. My father smiled as we talked and repeated what he says all the time of late: "I'm so proud to be with you." The maitre'd gave the roses to my father to hand to us. He handed the flowers to us, even though, as he did so, he said, "What are these for?"

As usual, he whistled between courses, but not too loudly. It was a pleasant evening. I thought of what it would have been like for my mother and father if they had been alone on what was supposed to be a romantic night filled with love and memories. The absence of memories of loving moments to share with my father might have made it a painful holiday for my mother if I hadn't been there.

She couldn't share memories with my father of the day they met or of what happened at their wedding. She couldn't share memories of their anniversaries or the births of their children or the marriages of their daughters or the births of their grandchildren. All that is gone from my father's brain. I came home to be the one she could remember with, even if I can only conjure up the way my mother's bouquet looked that day from the black and white photos. That night I thought about how strange it must be to feel so alone while you are still with someone, someone who can't remember your life together.

Chapter Eleven

The Daughter Track

Daughters like me who have come home to help their parents have developed a kind of divining rod that leads them home. An incident occurs—an emergency, or a parent is hospitalized or faces hospitalization soon. The caregiving spouse of the parent who is sick reaches the breaking point. Maybe we hear it in the tone of voice in a phone call from a mother or father, the unmistakable sound of a life crumbling, falling apart. A signal goes out, and suddenly we are packing our things and heading home.

We are not all single and childless. Some daughters I've talked with pack up kids and husbands to begin the trek home. Most of the time, they are not filling up empty lives or making up for meaningless careers. It is often quite the opposite. Many of them take on much more than they realistically should, and yet the pull home is undeniable.

I have talked with a woman who left an active life in the sunny Southwest, taking her two children with her to move in with her parents in a tiny town in the Midwest. Her life is sad and difficult these days as she continues to care for her ailing mother. She says her only consolation is the Harley she bought to help her deal with the death of her father. Yet she says she wouldn't have it any other way.

Another woman I interviewed moved her husband and young children back home to help her parents in Alabama. Her father died shortly after she arrived. Money is tight. She's trying to balance caregiving and her job as the sole breadwinner in the family. Her husband is ill as well as her mother, and they are all living together in the same home. We joked that she might as well hang a hospital shingle on her front door. However, each day she says she feels blessed.

A woman in Flint, Michigan, who moved her mother, who has Alzheimer's, into her home with her husband and daughter, deals with caregiving in an optimistic way: she sewed taps on her mother's bedroom slippers so she could tap dance along with the rest of the family as she sits in her chair.

In an article in the *New York Times* on November 24, 2005, journalist Jane Gross dubbed this new trend of women giving up careers or putting them on hold to take care of ailing parents "The Daughter Track."

Carole Levine, director of the Families and Health Care Project at the United Hospital Fund and an advisor to the National Alliance for Caregiving, says, "It's a safe assumption that women are more likely to put their careers on hold or end them because of caregiving responsibilities." Levine says it's hard to come up with a pat answer to the question of how many caregivers there are in the United States because organizations use different definitions for *caregiver*. Right now the figure her organization uses is "27 to 28 million caregivers in the U.S. The National Alliance for Caregiving uses a figure above 50 million, but I think that's generous. I feel more comfortable with the lower number. But that's still a lot." Levine says the biggest number of caregivers are "adult children; then it's spouses." She says often the people who need the care are "older women who have outlived their spouses. So it's often the adult children who become the caregivers. Sometimes also the spouse is ill and can't do the caregiving so an adult child steps in."

The Family Caregiver Alliance defines the term *caregiver* like this: "anyone who provides assistance to someone else who is, in some degree, incapacitated and needs help: a husband who has suffered a stroke; a wife with Parkinson's disease; a mother-in-law with cancer; a grandfather with Alzheimer's disease; a son with traumatic brain injury from a car accident; a child with muscular dystrophy; a friend with AIDS." The alliance says that in 2007 the number of informal and family caregivers combined was an estimated 52 million.

The Family Caregiver Alliance says that more women than men are caregivers. An estimated 59 to 70 percent of caregivers are female. The cost to replace women caregivers who quit their jobs because of their caregiving responsibilities is estimated at $3.3 billion.

Life can seem to come to a halt for some daughters who come home. For others, it's as if life begins. One thing is clear: daughters who move home to help aging parents find a new emotional and physical landscape. The markers they live by change. Some psyches survive the ordeal. Others do not. Daughters I talked with are of almost every age, ethnicity, and economic status. Perhaps the only thing they have in common is how much they love their parents.

Decarol Randle

Decarol Randle is one of the many daughters across the United States who took the extreme measure of moving in with an ailing parent. She had lived in Atlanta for seventeen years when her mother in Portland, Oregon, was diagnosed with dementia in August 2005. She says, "Initially, I came for two weeks to take my mother to a couple of doctor appointments. The same day I was scheduled to return to Atlanta, my sister placed our mother in a foster home without my knowledge or consent. When I discovered what my sister had done, I turned around and came back to remove my mother from the home where she'd been placed and to help her with her health issues."

Decarol moved without transportation, money, a job, or a plan. She says, "I had no idea how my mother and I were going to pay for anything. I altered clothing, made scarves, worked temp assignments, and was able to pay my personal bills every month. I was busy trying to find work, preparing healthy meals, going to doctor's appointments, and spending the remainder of my time trying to keep myself from slipping totally and completely into depression."

Since she came home, Decarol has tried to keep her mother healthy and improve the quality of her life. She says, "I keep her as active as possible by keeping her involved with the Urban League and other centers. I encourage family members and friends to come by and visit with her or to take her somewhere out of the house." She now works full time during the week and manages her mother's affairs, which includes speaking to her doctors. Decarol puts it like this: "I am the 'go to' girl for everything.

"I reside in the same home as my mother, and we don't get respite unless we can both afford it. There are many times when we both need a break from each other yet have to be around one another," Decarol says. "One of my friends says he admires me. I tell him not to, that I'm just trying to do what I can. I don't know that I've inspired anyone, but I have definitely learned a number of important points concerning caregiving: Take respite care often and whenever it's offered. Make time for yourself to do what you want. Try to arrange events or visits for the care recipient to be with her peers. Don't expect any help from your family; no one is coming to relieve you from this responsibility. Don't ignore your own health issues." Decarol adds: "Pray, pray, pray."

Decarol admits it is hard to have a social life in her situation. "I have very few friends in Portland and some acquaintances. Most of the people I speak to are my mother's friends, and it's usually about my mother and her status. I don't have a social life and haven't had one since I've been here. It is extremely taxing on your body, mind, and spirit to constantly cue someone to do things that well people do automatically. The amount of energy it drains from you is unbelievable. At the end of the day, it is just me and God."

Debra Roberts

Debra Roberts lives in New York City. She says before she moved into her mother's apartment to help take care of her, she already had a close relationship with her. "She helped me raise my son. She had a husband, but they didn't have a good marriage. I had to take over her care when she became ill. My sister also helped."

A series of events occurred at the same time that her mother got sick. "Two weeks before I lost my job to downsizing, I found out my mother had fourth-stage lung cancer that had metastasized to her brain. I didn't move in right away. I kept my apartment for three months, and then my son and I moved in with her. I lived with her for three years. My parents have a big apartment, a four-bedroom in a housing project. I became the primary caregiver."

Debra says her mother had no insurance. "She had brain surgery and then she had lung surgery, then she underwent radiation of the brain, then the chemo after lung surgery, then it went to her bones. She was in moderate pain, not terrible pain.

"I was able to talk with her up until the year 2000," Debra says. "The last year, she wasn't able to talk. My life was like this: I would take her out in the wheelchair by the mayor's park. We'd go and sit by the river. We had a nice time. We enjoyed each other. It was hard, but it was easy at the same time. It was a gift for me."

Debra says she basically swore off meeting friends. She says she felt like a monk in a monastery. "I didn't socialize. I had my son so I was trying to be a caregiver and be a mom for him, too. I had my sister. I never socialized that much in the first place so I was able to adapt to that lifestyle." I asked her if she went to support groups or if she established any other sort of network to help her out. "I went to spiritual services on Sundays. To stay sane, I exercised. I cooked and meditated. I focused more on my internal rather than my external being. It gave me peace. I'm basically an easygoing, happy spirit.

"There were lots of doctor's appointments and hospitals. But you know, I was the one she wanted. She wanted me to take care of her. I was the one who was most willing and able to take care of her. A lot of people can't be around sick people. In a way, it was perfect timing. It really was."

Debra says, "She would sleep a lot. She would fall out of her bed. I ended up sleeping with her. She didn't want a stranger in the house taking care of her. She's very proud. German. They want their own around!" Debra says her mother's final days were difficult but touching and sweet at the same time. "She died in her apartment. We had hospice the two days before she died. They gave her a morphine patch."

Her mother was sixty-five years old when she died in July 2001. Debra got what so many of the daughters I've talked with want but aren't always able to achieve—being able to make their mother or father feel loved in the last years of their lives despite illness or pain, and giving them tenderness at the time of death.

When she looks back on the time spent taking care of her mother, Debra says, "For some reason, I wanted to do it all. It all blended in very well. It was my way of giving back to my mom. She had given so much to me." The last thing Debra said to me was, "I was a designated daughter."

Terina Ditto

Terina Ditto speaks in a lovely, lilting southern drawl. Her words slip and slide like silver. She takes her time. You can tell she is a woman who lives by her own rules and has made her own life decisions, regardless of what others think.

It was difficult for me to set up a time to interview Terina because of various health problems her family was facing. I told her we could reschedule the interview when things returned to normal. She laughed and told me, "Things are never normal here! Normal is just a setting on the dryer!"

Terina moved her husband and three kids in with her mother and father after they learned that her father had congestive heart failure and had only six months to live. Her mother had an inoperable brain tumor that made her unable to take care of herself alone. Her father had been taking care of her mother by himself for several years.

Like other caregivers I've talked with, Terina found herself putting lots of miles on her car driving back and forth from Atlanta to Montgomery to take her mother and father to the doctor. The long caregiving commute and the worry when she wasn't there forced a decision.

She says, "We finally just decided to move here. My husband always wanted to have his own woodworking shop. And so he decided he could do that anywhere. I was a stay-at-home mom for twenty years, and so we moved over here."

Terina's father's doctor predicted he had only six months to live and recommended that the family call in hospice. "I had a teenage daughter and a son who was in the second grade. My oldest was in college. And we all just moved in with them so I could be there to take care of him and because he couldn't take care of my mother alone anymore."

Again I asked the question I asked of so many daughters: How did she become the designated one? "I was the youngest. I was the baby of the family," Terina says. "But I always felt responsible for them. I keep noticing that caregivers are mostly daughters.

"I had never thought of myself as a strong person. I always thought I was dependent. But all of a sudden I was cast into this role of taking care of everybody. I don't know how I ended up here. I guess nobody else could do it. It wasn't a conscious decision." Terina says her caregiving role surprised her "because I never thought of myself as a strong person. I used to question God and say, 'God, you picked the wrong person!'"

One of the most difficult parts in this role Terina has found herself in is, "You have to be there for everybody. This stuff about taking care of yourself—I'm definitely lacking in this area. I don't eat right. I have that personality that says, 'How hard can it be?'" She says that, like many daughters, she probably didn't realize how much work it would be to take care of a dying father and a sick mother.

"I didn't think of it as a sacrifice at the time. It seemed like the natural thing to do." However difficult it was, Terina says she has no regrets about moving home to help take care of her father and mother.

Terina says she feels privileged to have been with her father as he died. "I literally slept with him at night. We had long talks. We talked and talked. I learned so much about him and about myself and about the dying process. It's not like in the movies. It's not pretty. It's a lot of waiting. And a lot of patience."

Terina's life is an example of the many medical problems and other symptoms that fall like dominos for caregivers. It often begins with one sick parent. Then another parent—often an exhausted caregiver spouse—gets ill, too. That's when a daughter or son or other caregiver steps in and must be on call twenty-four hours a day. Jobs and relationships begin to fall by the wayside. The next thing a caregiver knows, he or she is caught in a merry-go-round of caregiving, dealing with a mother and/or father's hospitalization, recovery, and illness, which makes the caregiver's life come to a halt or change immensely. Sometimes, when it's all over, the caregiver is unable to get his or her own life back.

Terina's mother is now eighty-three years old with an inoperable brain stem tumor and various impairments from strokes. "She can't see or hear well, and she walks with a walker. She has trouble eating. I puree her food. She can't swallow anything that's not soft or ground up. My mother has home health that comes in a couple of days a week for bathing. That has been a tremendous help. My husband gets home in the afternoon to help, too."

I asked Terina, "Are you glad you did this?" "I am," she said immediately. But then she admitted, "I feel sorry for myself sometimes. I say, I'm not the person for this job. You need someone a lot smarter and a lot better. But there are so many people who lost their mother at a young age. I know this is a blessing, and I know I will look back and I will feel thankful for this time."

Daughters who have come home to help in the care of one or both of their aging parents are faced with a jumble of emotions. The first one is often a feeling of gratitude and a sense that they are giving back after all the things their parents have done for them. They feel generous, good of heart, and kind at the get-go. Then, after more than year, for some of the daughters I talked with, the good feelings sometimes morph into anger, resentment, guilt, or a feeling of being trapped or stuck. Those are the most common words many of the women I talked with use after they've been helping sick parents for a significant amount of time.

The more people I talked with, the clearer I became that I have it easy, so much easier than most.

Mike Gamble

More daughters than sons come home to help their ailing parents. According to the Family Caregiver Alliance, 59 to 75 percent of caregivers are women. Although some studies have indicated a growing percentage of male caregivers, the more demanding care responsibilities (bathing, toileting, hands-on medical care) still fall primarily to wives, daughters, and other women caregivers. But male caregivers are out there, and their number is expected to increase as the aging population and the number of people with diseases such as Alzheimer's continues to grow.

Mike Gamble is the president, CEO, and founder of Senior Solutions of America, Inc. His Web site, Aging Parents and Elder Care (www.aging-parents-and-elder-care.com), offers a support group to which many of the daughters I interviewed go to vent. Quite a few of the caregiving daughters told me they wish they could see a therapist on a regular basis, but they simply don't have the time or the money. So after a tough day of caregiving and sometimes working a full- or part-time job, they go to their computers to seek solace, comfort, and a community to help them through these stressful times. Mike Gamble tells me he founded his company and the support group that came out of it after his own experiences taking care of his mother and father.

Mike says he'll never forget the time he flew from Chicago where he lived with his wife and children to visit his parents in Florida. "Dad was sitting at the kitchen table with me and he virtually broke down. He said, 'I simply can't care for your mom anymore.'" He says his mother "had a broken pelvis, osteoporosis, she had a heart attack in 1990, spinal fusion, two or three vertebrae with steel rods. She was on all sorts of drugs and medications. She had spent thirteen days at the hospital comatose."

Like many adult children, Mike felt he had to step in to help because "our parents placed doctors on pedestals. [My mother] was sitting on the couch all day long oblivious to what was going on. She paced all night long. Dad's health was deteriorating." He says his father had a host of health problems, too. "He had gone through physical therapy. He was losing strength. He was a very intelligent man. He was president of his own sales organization. But he never was good at asking for help." Mike explains that he and his siblings "investigated bringing in a home health care agency. We had a couple of aides come in to help him after he had fallen down." His parents' health care crisis continued in a downward spiral. His father had a stroke and then died.

This is when he realized firsthand the amount of work involved in helping to take care of sick parents. In his own career in the health care field, Mike says, "I had been dealing with Medicare and other elder care issues since 1966. But little did I know . . ."

Shortly after his father died, his mother fell and broke her hip. His family placed her in a nursing home, and that's when Mike says he and the doctors began to realize that some of his mother's problems were caused by the effects of the drugs she was taking. He says, "We gradually weaned her off some drugs and she started coming back mentally." However, at that point his mother had already suffered brain damage.

He was coordinating his mother's health care from Chicago and getting down to Florida to help whenever he could. He says, "You have to manage your parents' health care or you get nasty surprises." One of those nasty surprises turned out to be that the facility where he had placed his mother cost $120,000 a year.

Mike says one of the things that worried him most was "the prescriptions were all wrong. If I hadn't been there, who knows what could have happened. In my own experience, it's the predominant way elder care is handled. The adult children better get off of their duffs. These kids better realize that it may be inconvenient to help their mom or dad, but it seems to me now the shoe is on the other foot."

Many of the people who use Mike's Web site have been forced to become patient advocates for their sick parents. "You have to have questions," Mike says. "You have to have follow-up. Be a squeaky wheel. And remember: honey works better than a stick."

The people who use Mike's Web site are "usually women who can feel free to come there and unload. People talk about a variety of situations and they can get advice. It's a way they help each other." There's a "bulletin board, a support group. It's like a chat room." The Web site also offers 150 to 200 pages of information on aspects related to caregiving. Mike says, "I'm trying to cover the entire spectrum. It does make me feel good that I've provided a place for people to go. A lot of these women hit the nail on the head when they tell each other, 'You have to place the caregiver first.' Her life must be first, because otherwise the caregiver will not have the energy to provide the care to the person who needs it."

Many caregivers seem unable to take Mike's advice. Mike says of the support group on his Web site: "Those who are in difficult caregiving situations need a place to vent where they're not going to be prejudged. They're talking with people in similar situations, in situations like their own." People in the chat room engage in problem solving and offer advice. Often a daughter or son will describe what he or she is experiencing and simply write, "I'm in this situation. Can anybody help?" Mike says one of the advantages is the anonymity of his Web site.

Mike is seeing a trend of more and more adult children coming home to help their aging parents instead of taking the step of putting their loved ones in nursing homes. He explains that this is because of distrust of the care given by doctors, nursing homes, and hospitals. He believes, as in his own situation, that if a patient advocate or an adult child didn't come to the aid of ailing parents to make sure they get the proper medical care and treatment, many of them would die much faster.

On the Aging Parents and Elder Care Web site, adult children write about their extreme emotional distress. Sometimes they vent about the financial drain of taking care of ailing parents. Some ask legal and medical questions, which people in the support group try to answer. At any given moment, you can peruse the Web site and read about a variety of problems from a host of people in pain and witness a number of people helping each other out.

Yet even on a Web site where bitching is allowed, even encouraged, you still see wonderful things—a person saying how glad he or she is to have had this time to help a parent and share this time in his or her life.

Ami Simms

Ami Simms, who lives in Flint, Michigan, is a quilter by profession. She gives lectures, teaches workshops, and leads quilting classes across the globe. She has written eight books about quilting. She has also applied a lot of her creative and artistic energy to taking care of her mother who has Alzheimer's, and to helping to raise money to find a cure for the disease.

Ami has patched together her own system of caregiving the way she stitches one of her quilts: she made her own rules. "There was no question," she says. "If my mother couldn't take care of herself, that was our job." Before her mother was diagnosed, she and her husband, with input from her mother, designed their house with her mother in mind. They built a special apartment attached to their home in preparation for the day an older, potentially disabled mother might move in. The large bathrooms, extra-wide closets and stairways, grab bars—everything was in place. At the time, Alzheimer's wasn't even on their minds.

"We thought for sure it would be a physical disability, not anything mental," Ami says. "We thought we had done this tremendous planning, but we hadn't even thought about a cognitive disability." After her mother had had a series of memory problems, trouble with driving, then dangerous driving, including a left-hand turn from a left-hand turn lane that didn't exist (she was trying to turn from the fast lane), Ami finally took her mother to a doctor in 2001. The diagnosis: Alzheimer's. Shortly afterward, her mother moved in with Ami, her husband, and her daughter.

Ami created a caregiving team that consisted of her family and the employees who helped to run her quilting business from her

home. She says her family and her employees took a positive, in-
clusive approach from the very beginning. "We gave [my mother]
something to sew or patch every day. We said, 'Look, you make
beautiful patchwork. Why don't you do that, and we'll find somebody who can sell it to charity?' She would either dye or stamp
fabric or make quilts or make clothes. She probably made fabric
for three hundred charity quilts." Ami says that despite her Alzheimer's, her mother worked with fabric every day.

Ami says of the impact on her and her family: "I never could
have imagined how much having my mom live with us would
change our lives. It happened in small, incremental steps. Each of
us started taking on tasks she couldn't do anymore. It was like one
grain of sand followed by another grain of sand. But this is very
easy to do for someone you love so much."

Ami started incorporating her feelings about her mother's Alzheimer's into her quilts. "I decided to create art about Alzheimer's. I wanted to do a piece that would portray Alzheimer's: dark
black threads grinding into the fabric and obliterating all the
beauty of the patchwork. It was an angry quilt. From there, I
began thinking about curating an exhibit that would feature quilts
about Alzheimer's made by other artists. At the same time, I was
asking for donation quilts we could sell to raise money for Alzheimer's research." As of summer 2007, Ami had raised $75,000
for the Alzheimer's Association, which is earmarked for research.
(You can learn more about Ami and the Alzheimer's quilt initiative
at www.AlzQuilts.org.)

Ami says she always tried to approach her mother's disease in an
optimistic way. When she and several friends decided to take tap
dancing lessons, "We actually created the Flint Area Recreational
Tapdancing Society (FARTS) so we could all tap dance together.
I sewed taps to the bottoms of [my mother's] bedroom slippers
because of balance issues. So she tapped with us from a seated
position."

Would Ami recommend moving a parent living with Alzheimer's into one's home the way she did? "I'm so glad I did this. It's what you do. How could I not?" Ami says, "Everybody's experiences are different. Everybody's relationship with their parent is different. You have to do what's right for your family. There are no rules here."

But Ami says, "I wish I could have done more."

How do you become the one that comes home, or the one who has your mother or father move in with you or your family? Daughters I have talked with who have done what I have done seem to share the feeling that they felt designated from the beginning. Because I wasn't married and didn't have children, I didn't have to sacrifice as much as my sisters would have. But there is more. Many of the daughters I have talked with felt a close bond with their mother or father, as I did. There is also an inexplicable pull home that many of us seem to share. Some believe it is a kind of spiritual journey we're called to undertake. That is what it has been for me. When I was in San Francisco and in New York, something seemed to be pulling me home. It took me some time to hear the words and answer the call.

Since I came home, I have learned so many things about myself I didn't know before. I have developed skills I didn't know I had, and a new kind of patience. I have discovered a whole new plateau of love. (I have also begun to learn how to play tennis and how to use Oxyclean, but that is another story.)

If I had stayed with my job as a broadcast journalist, I believe I would have grown in my career, but perhaps not in my personal life. My life looked "evolved" from the outside, but I was at a standstill in so many ways. All I defined myself by was my work. There was a lesson I needed to learn that, in some ways, my job was keeping me from.

I think I moved so fast (and drank so much coffee) and rushed to each breaking news story, trying to be the first one on scene, so that I could keep from being pinned down by anyone. My job helped me to avoid having deep relationships or deep bonds with others. When I look back on the way I worked over the past twenty years, I believe I subconsciously used my job to avoid intimacy.

Now, instead of trying to get out of a situation that would force me to deal with deep love or great sadness, by coming home to help take care of my father and to be with my mother, I ran *toward* grief, instead of running away. Unlike the way I led my life before, I am facing it. I am looking it in the eye. I am not using my career as a reason to get out of dealing with my relationships. By coming home, instead of pretending things are okay or being in denial, I was saying, This is what we must face, this sadness, this pain, this injury to our family, this slow death. By facing it, I hope I am helping my mother and my entire family face it, too.

I am ensconced in the intimacy of grief from the moment I wake up until I go to sleep. Each day, even though there is a lot of pain, I am also rewarded by the feeling I am helping someone as well.

The other day, I was helping my father take a shower. My mother was enjoying a bit of time off so I was the sole caregiver for several hours. I put out my father's clothes on his bed and began running the shower. After putting out his shampoo and soap, I started helping him take off his undershirt. He completed the task of undressing himself. With no apparent self-consciousness, shyness, or awkwardness, he took off his undershorts. There he was standing naked just a few feet from me. At first my reaction was, This shouldn't be happening. This can't be happening. But there was a task at hand. I simply helped my naked father into the shower. Then I had what I would consider an out-of-body experience.

It was as if I could look down on myself doing this. It was so foreign, and yet in moments it seemed so routine. The moment changed from uncomfortable to innocent and almost beautiful.

For a moment I thought, I can't believe it has come to this. Seconds later, I realized this was an honor.

How did this happen? How is it that my father is allowing me to be this close to him, trusting me to take care of him, to take him to the next stage of his life, to see him naked as he enters the shower? How did he and I offer this up to each other in the scheme of things? How did I come to be the one to do this? How did it get to this point? How did the tether let go and drop me off here?

This disease is destroying my father, and yet it is helping me take an emotional leap to a new level of love. At times I think that as this disease destroys my father, it strengthens me. My father is helping me to find my way home to my heart.

I realize now that in coming home and participating fully in the decline of my father, I have been forced to face my own life, my own feelings, my own fears, my own failures and strengths. And yet at the same time, I have shifted the markers in my life to my parents'. This could be dangerous, because when they are gone, the markers I live by will be gone.

There is definitely a downside to having come home to help care for my father. There is something unsettling about telling the person you are dating that you spent the afternoon riding motorized shopping carts with your father through a department store. I noticed recently that I am beginning to lose my connection to popular culture after being immersed in it for so many years. Not only did I miss the birth of Shiloh (the daughter of Hollywood celebrities Brad Pitt and Angelina Jolie), but I didn't even care about it. I didn't even know a joke about it the way I would have if I had been in a newsroom. I don't have an iPod. I don't *want* to have an iPod. And if I had one, I might not be able to work it.

My friends Michaelynn and Suzy call from San Francisco. They've been to Stinson Beach or to the opera. They've been to the Saturday morning farmer's market at the Ferry Building on the bay, where we used to meet, or to a controversial documentary at the Castro Theatre or to an avante garde play. My friends in New York report on the latest Broadway show, what's at the Met or at Lincoln Center, or a musician they saw perform in Greenwich Village. I have nothing to report to them, however, except things like "Dad drank his Ensure today," or, "I clipped my father's fingernails." I noticed the other day that my speech patterns have changed. I vaguely remember the hyper, fast-talking person that I was. Now, I talk more slowly so my father can understand.

My friends' lives in the cities I left seem so big. My life seems so small. Yet I feel connected to the world in a larger way than I have before. I won't pretend there aren't times I long to look once again from my rooftop on Telegraph Hill over the city of San Francisco, to see the sunset turn the buildings golden or the Bay Bridge sparkling at night. Sometimes I even miss my pager going off at 2 a.m. or the racket of the Roosevelt Island tram going by my apartment in New York on Sixty-first and First in the middle of the night. I often long to drive to the wine country for the weekend or take a walk through Central Park, the things I used to do in my former life.

You wake up one morning, and you realize you are living the life your parents are living. You start looking forward to watching the *The NewsHour with Jim Lehrer* on public television and pouring a glass of wine at 6 p.m. Perhaps the most shocking thing of all is that you actually look forward to heading to bed by 9 or 10 p.m.

The benefits are that your heart expands. You find out who you are when you stop moving so fast. You retrace some of your life and try to get it right this time. You go through old photos with your mother and learn more about your family and where you came from. You sit by the fire with her in a way you never had time to before. You get to know who she is, and you hear about the small town where your grandfather grew up. You realize what you're made of. You provide comfort for both your parents in a way you never could before. You get permission to slow down.

In the end, you know you've made a difference in your parents' lives when they needed you most. Each morning when you wake up, you know you'll be helping someone you love get through their day.

A woman friend of mine told me about a man she met at an event in New York. I said, "Oh my God, you wouldn't actually consider going out with him, would you? I mean, he's such a nerd! He's fifty years old and he still lives with his parents!" I stopped in my tracks. I froze. Then we started laughing. I had completely forgotten: I am one of those middle-aged nerds who lives with her parents.

Some of us dreamed of home for so long. Now many of us are dreaming of a way out. Many of us are waking up in either unknown territory or territory we have traveled many, many times before: our childhood homes. When I first came home, I woke up in the middle of the night in a cold sweat, searching for the symbols and signs of my life in San Francisco, Los Angeles, or New York. These days, that doesn't happen. The other day I realized I don't want those things to identify me anymore.

Daughters like me are redefining the role of caregiver. We aren't coming home because we have to, but because we want to. We're coming home to help our parents and to help ourselves. We are coming home to find something we lost along the way.

Chapter Twelve

Where to Turn

IF THERE IS NO FAMILY MEMBER TO come home to help take care of a person living with Alzheimer's the way I did, who is out there to help? Sometimes I wish some sort of team would move in to come to the aid of people like my parents. Right now, so many people who discover that Alzheimer's is part of their lives feel left out in the cold.

It turns out there *is* help available in many communities across the United States. The difficult part for people like my mother is reaching out to get it. The Alzheimer's Association is often the first place caregivers call for help. Dian Wilkins, president and CEO of the Alzheimer's Association's Greater Michigan chapter, has been helping people living with Alzheimer's and their caregivers for twenty years.

"Some physicians refer [people] to us," Wilkins said. "Sometimes families call us first. We have a twenty-four hour help line (800-272-3900, www.alz.org) with social workers on duty. We will counsel them on the phone. We have a full array of services. We might determine on the phone they need in-person counseling or care management or care consultation. Perhaps the caregiver needs a support group. Perhaps they want to come to one of our adult day care programs. That initial intake, that point of entry on the telephone—the twenty-four-hour help line—that's a crucial piece, because from there we can funnel them to various services within our agency or outside our agency. If they don't have a diagnosis yet, we can refer them to a physician who's a geriatric specialist. If they need a nursing home, we have those lists. We can refer them to other services—if they need an attorney for elder care legal issues such as guardianship, medical power of attorney, all of that kind of thing."

The Alzheimer's Association is one-stop shopping for all things Alzheimer's, but Dian Wilkins and others at the association feel that not enough people use their resources.

My mother isn't the type to call a twenty-four-hour help line late at night. In fact, she isn't one to ask for help from anyone, even in the bright light of day. I have wondered why my mother didn't take advantage of all the services offered by the Alzheimer's Association the minute she and my father learned my father had been diagnosed with the disease.

Marcia Mittleman, education and training director for the Alzheimer's Association's Greater Michigan chapter, has a theory: "My experience has been—and I've been working with older adults all my life—that many times there's a stage of denial. We kind of cover up. 'Really the symptoms aren't that bad,' 'They're still able to get by.' They might still be driving, or they laugh it off, and they still have their social graces."

Mittleman says denial can run so deep that the person living with Alzheimer's doesn't get the medical help he or she needs. The caregiver avoids getting the help he or she needs, too, because to reach out for help means admitting what's happening to your family. You have to admit that your life is being torn apart by Alzheimer's, and many people have a hard time doing that.

Mittleman suggests, "Number one: make sure to get the proper diagnosis, because there are over sixty types of dementia. The key is early intervention. The drugs on the market are most effective in the early stages. I think also there's a societal issue: we don't want to talk about Alzheimer's. We don't want to deal with it." She says families avoid going to the doctor, going to a therapist, going to support groups, and even asking their own loved ones for help because it's a way to pretend it isn't happening. It's a way to keep the beast of Alzheimer's at bay.

"Usually what happens," Mittleman says, "is that it's going to be a crisis. The person with dementia is driving and they don't know where they are, or there's another wake-up call. There's something wrong." Mittleman says often it is a crisis that gets the family to call for help from the Alzheimer's Association, a doctor, adult day care, respite care, support groups, or a therapist.

Mittleman says that caregivers avoid getting the help they need for a variety of reasons. "You personalize it. You say, 'Why can't I take care of everything? I'm the caregiver and that's my role; that's my job. If I can't do it, I'm a failure. I'm letting him down.'"

According to Dian Wilkins, another factor in caregivers putting off getting help is stoicism. When my mother and father got married in 1950, they took their wedding vows very seriously. "We hear that a lot," Wilkins says. "[People say,] 'I made a commitment. We made a promise. We talked about this. I promised I'd never put him in a home.' I think it does have to do with the era and the role of women when they got married. It's just ingrained, trained into us: we are the caregiver no matter what. And there's denial."

Because of all the psychological and social factors that kick in when someone has Alzheimer's, it is often difficult to connect services with the people who need them. Every family starts from scratch on the caregiving track and makes its own rules along the way. Every family is left to its own devices, no matter how ill equipped, until family members get the courage to ask for help. For some, asking for help is the most difficult step of all.

Is it my mother's pride and desire for self-sufficiency that is keeping her out of the loop of receiving help from others besides her therapist and me? I wonder whether I have become some sort of gatekeeper. Because I am here, have I prevented her from reaching out to others who could have helped her along the way and perhaps given her more help than I can give? I sometimes worry that my coming home has prevented her from getting the professional respite she needs and maybe even facing the fact that it may be time for my father to go to a residential facility where he can be cared for by experts all day long.

In a January 1999 report in the *Journal of the American Medical Association*, Richard Schulz, PhD, and Scott R. Beach, PhD, described their study of 392 caregivers and 427 noncaregivers aged sixty-six to ninety-six who were living with their spouses. They wanted to find out more about the impact of caregiving demands. The study was conducted from 1993 through 1998. After four years of follow-up, 103 participants (12.6 percent) had died. After adjusting for sociodemographic factors, prevalent disease, and subclinical cardiovascular disease, the researchers determined that participants who were providing care and experiencing caregiver strain had mortality risks that were 63 percent higher than those of noncaregiving controls. The researchers concluded the following: "Our study suggests that being a caregiver who is experiencing mental or emotional strain is an independent risk factor for mortality among elderly spousal caregivers. Caregivers who report strain associated with caregiving are more likely to die than noncaregiving controls."

There is no doubt that caregivers are at risk of losing not only their mental health but also their physical health. Yet many caregivers, like my mother, forget that neglecting their own needs may actually be putting their lives at risk.

You have to create your own plan each day to deal with the needs of the person living with Alzheimer's because those needs change every day. One day I had what seemed like a pretty nice day plotted out. My father, however, decided the throbbing pulse on the right side of his forehead meant that he was near death. "I'm dying!" he exclaimed over and over as he touched the place on his temple where he could feel the blood pumping, something a person living with Alzheimer's might not be able to comprehend. I couldn't do the things I thought I was going to do because he needed me to help him through a very bad stage. I had to sit next to him, get ice for his head, and try to talk him down. I said, "Everyone has a pulse like that. I do, too." I explained this to him over and over and told him he was not dying. The next thing I knew it was 5 p.m. and the day was shot. Incidents like this have happened to my mother, over and over again, over a period of many years. This is how one's life gets hijacked by Alzheimer's.

There's no doubt that support groups work for many people, but they didn't seem to fit for my mother or for me. We attended a support group together not long after I came home. It was useful for many of the people in the group, and we shared resources and gave each other support and understanding. But my sense was that it didn't give my mother what she needed. She had no desire to go back. Neither did I. My mother attended another Alzheimer's support group shortly after my father was diagnosed. She said the facilitator started the meeting by reading the names of people associated with the group who had died from the disease. The meeting was mainly about health insurance and wills. It was probably helpful to people who hadn't considered these issues, but she had. For her, the meeting only made her depressed. At that point, she said, she didn't need to get any more "down" than she already was.

At one of the support groups we attended, a woman explained at length what it was like to help her father who has Alzheimer's put his dentures in. Another woman described the way she diapered her mother. I believe it is important to be able to vent and to listen to the venting, and to share the pain and sorrow, but we're not at the helping-with-dentures-and-diapering stage yet. For now, anyway, we have decided that rather than talk about how awful it is, we'd rather celebrate the good parts of our lives—and my father's life—while we still have them. Clearly, we have more good times than many people who take care of people living with Alzheimer's.

Magazines such as *Caring Today*, which was created specifically to meet the needs of caregivers (I am on the editorial advisory board), can help people like my mother and me. We can open the pages when we need to. We can take advice in our own time (even at 3 a.m.). We can implement advice, or not, take it or leave it or file it away to use later on. (We can also go to the Web site at www.car ingtoday.com.)

The Alzheimer's Association offers online information and support groups, too, that can be accessed any time at www.alz.org. As mentioned earlier, the Web site at www.aging-parents-and-elder-care.com is a comprehensive resource for family caregivers during all stages of care.

Carolyn McIntyre, a psychotherapist and social worker, specializes in dealing with families affected by Alzheimer's. Her mother was diagnosed with Alzheimer's in 1991. McIntyre says, "Different families respond different ways [to learning that a family member has Alzheimer's]. A tight, enmeshed family comes together quickly. A disengaged family will have a harder time. Every family is different. There's a different culture and a different style. The family usually comes together around diagnosis or hospitalization or an accident. There's also denial. A lot of us don't want to see our parents as sick and needy. We want to see them as strong, and the role change is difficult."

McIntyre says that Alzheimer's disease requires an unusual kind of grief. "First, you have to grieve the person you once knew. With Alzheimer's, you're saying good-bye and then the person doesn't leave. And Alzheimer's is only going to get progressively worse. Other illnesses are episodic, and then they might stabilize. With Alzheimer's, the family has a hard time getting used to it."

McIntyre says there's no pat response to Alzheimer's disease. "Everyone doesn't need therapy, but they do need outside resources—

doctors, nurses, aides, a health care attendant. We used the Al-zheimer's Association, and we met with a social worker. We got some support and attended lectures. We learned about legal issues and got a health care proxy. If the caregiver doesn't have power of attorney, there are problems. But giving over control is very hard for many parents. Some parents are stubborn about accepting out-side help, even to get a housecleaner in the home."

McIntyre says that support groups can help by just allowing the caregiver and the family a place to vent. She says, "Disease-specific groups are good. There are online things you can do, too, as well as seeing a therapist or psychiatrist." She adds, "It's very typical for the caregivers not to worry about themselves. You have to remind them to take care of themselves. There is a prevalence of physical and mental problems for the caregiver."

The 2006 Evercare Study of Caregivers in Decline found that "Caregivers say that they would care more about themselves if someone conveyed that they care about them. They say if a 'health coach' elicited personal commitment from them to do a particular health behavior, they would be more likely to follow through. Even simple reminders about their medical appointments or to eat right may help them keep their own health as a priority."

Often, sons and daughters come home as much for the caregiver as for the person living with Alzheimer's. We also do it for ourselves.

Chapter Thirteen

When Is It Time?

Spring 2007—that's when our family started seriously considering whether it might be time. We had been avoiding this discussion for so long—the discussion about placing my father in a residential care facility.

Taking care of my father is becoming too difficult for my mother, for me, and for my whole family. It is more than the constant, pervasive depression of being with someone who doesn't know much of anything anymore, more than the in-your-face grief of being with a husband and a father who is not the person he once was. It is hard to explain what seems like a breaking point. It is partly that he doesn't know objects these days. Though he can still sing, his speech is falling away. He can't do much of anything for himself, though he still folds laundry and vacuums. Because he can't understand instructions and doesn't know what most objects are, we can't really include him in many activities. When he's not at adult day care, his days are often spent watching television and whistling.

I feel lately that he would have a much better life being in a facility with activities and people all around him, where it is social, where there is music, and where people could take care of him and keep him stimulated all day long. Many people cannot afford to put a person living with Alzheimer's in a residential facility; they have no choice but to keep their loved one home, putting their mental and physical health in danger. But for those of us who *can* afford expert care, how do we tell when it's time? My mother will make the final decision. But here is what I know: I can't do it anymore.

In their booklet *Moving a Relative with Memory Loss: A Family Caregiver's Guide*, Beth Spencer and Laurie White say that making the decision to move depends on your personal situation. According to Spencer and White, many caregivers move their loved ones to a residential care facility for one or more of the following reasons:

- The amount of supervision and assistance needed by the relative with memory loss is too exhausting for the caregiver.
- The person with memory loss is no longer safe in his or her current residence.
- The caregiver is unable to keep up with both family and work responsibilities.
- Emergency and crisis situations for the caregiver or the person with memory loss have arisen.
- The current level of services is not enough, is too expensive, or is too difficult to arrange and sustain.

It's the first reason they list that is beginning to ring so true for us. Exhaustion. That's what my mother and I feel when we are alone with my father.

I talked with Beth Spencer in June 2007. She's a licensed master social worker and director of the Silver Club programs at the Geriatric Center at the University of Michigan in Ann Arbor. The Silver Club was started in 1998 as an adult day program specifically for people with dementia. She has spent most of her life working with people living with Alzheimer's and helping their caregivers. She says that just twenty years ago, "caregivers were totally neglected and desperate for information. They were very stressed. There were very few places for them to talk with people."

According to Spencer, caregivers are getting more help these days, especially since the inception and growth of the Alzheimer's Association. "I think we've come really a long way, but not far enough," she says. "I still see programs and nursing homes and assisted living where people are really ignorant about how to better serve the individual with dementia and how to talk to them about their needs and feelings and build on that. Medical care is certainly better. There are many more resources available."

Spencer and co-author Laurie White started a private practice called Caregiver Connection in Ann Arbor. One of the specific tasks they perform is to help families move their loved ones with Alzheimer's into nursing homes. "People asked us to give talks. We decided to compile our joint wisdom. That's how the book was born," Spencer said. I asked her to explain how families decide it's time to move someone with Alzheimer's out of the home.

"I don't think there's a right answer to that," she said. "When I'm giving talks on this, I say, 'Every family is different.' There are families that keep people home until the end of their life. I'm not sure it's the best choice. There may be a right time for a given family, but it's not the same as the next family. There are so many factors." Some of the factors to examine, she says, include: "How many people are available to help with the caregiving? Are they on their own or with one person? It takes a village to take care of someone with dementia."

Spencer asserts that, often, "It also comes down to finances, so that moving may be contingent on that. Often what's happening with the person's ability to sleep, certain behaviors, and just the general progression of the disease and other medical conditions will all play into that decision, especially when the caregiver is just so stressed."

Spencer told me a story about a caregiver she had been counseling and how she knew it might be time for that caregiver to take the person she loved with Alzheimer's to an institution. "She said to me, 'I wish he would just die.' I said, 'I understand that, but what that means is you're at the end of your rope. There may be a different mode of caregiving that you need now.'"

Caregivers also must consider how well a person with late-stage Alzheimer's will be able to acclimate to a new facility. It's often better to move the person sooner than later. "Here's one argument that I often use that most spouses have not thought about," Spencer says. "If he moves now versus later, he has a much better chance of developing relationships with other people in the facility and with staff members, participating in activities, becoming comfortable. If you wait another year or two or three, it may be much harder for him to move. He'll be more impaired."

For instance, if my family chose to move my father to a facility today, he would be seen as the sweet, singing Woody that he is now, a man able to introduce himself, feed himself, and even socialize somewhat. He would be able to develop relationships with others that would help sustain him and keep him stimulated.

Spencer says a big factor in the decision to move someone with Alzheimer's to residential care is the survival of the caregiver. "It's a terribly isolating disease for the person living with Alzheimer's and for the caregiver." She says it's often difficult for caregivers to realize that even when the person living with Alzheimer's moves to a residential facility, the relationship with the person continues. "You can choose to be involved to the extent that you want to. Your mom could be there during a meal, or she can do whatever gives her some sense of comfort, having a little bit more of a life for herself. The relationship gets easier. She's no longer the person who has to help him with bathing or dressing."

I asked Spencer to describe what options are open for people like my father. "The options are very much dependent on finances and geography and the physical abilities and disabilities of the person. For some people, adult foster care homes are a good option. They are small residential homes sometimes with six people or less. They're in a residential community, and they tend to be less expensive. They don't have much in the way of activities, and staffing is minimal. Some are memory-care specific."

Spencer says, "There are plenty of spouses who have a really hard time with the next step. Often, they just don't look realistically at what's happening. They're trying so desperately to hang on to the person that's there." She says spouses just can't fathom taking their loved one to a residential facility because "they feel like they are violating their wedding vows." Spencer tries to get the message out to spouses that taking a person with Alzheimer's to a nursing home, memory care facility, or assisted living is not The End. "This doesn't mean you're giving up on him. It doesn't mean you're dumping him somewhere. You're looking at a different way of caring for him. You just can't do it by yourself anymore. They've created environments especially for dealing with people who have Alzheimer's. You are still a caregiver. You are still a spouse. It's just a different role."

My family reads countless books on Alzheimer's disease. We read pamphlets describing "the next step." We get brochures about nursing homes and other residential facilities. We talk with doctors, social workers, and geriatric experts. But no one can tell you when it's time, because no one but us, and especially my mother, is an expert on Woody. That's why it is in my mother's hands to decide.

Why is it so hard for us to make this decision? Because there are still moments when he's on the tennis court lobbing a ball over the net or throwing a Frisbee to his grandsons, when he's in a restaurant toasting with a glass of wine and smiling, when he's singing with his a cappella singing group, performing his solo perfectly, and my family thinks, How could he go somewhere else? But in those moments, I realize that my mother is looking only at *his* life, not hers. Perhaps we all are.

I tried to fill up the empty spaces. I tried to get her out more to see people, to give her time alone, but the exhausting times with him are making her unable to enjoy her life much anymore or even to pursue other interests. Woody is her only concern, her only job these days. She does things for him that may appear senseless because he doesn't know or doesn't remember. She still takes him to parties, restaurants, concerts, and many other events, despite how difficult it is to get him there. Some say it isn't worth it anymore. She keeps doing these things to pretend that the man she once knew is in there somewhere, but the more she does them, the more exhausted she becomes.

Lately my mother admits there are days she feels she simply can't take care of him anymore, such as "on days when he holds his head, feeling his pulse, saying over and over again, 'There's something bad. There's something wrong. I'm terribly sick. I want to go to bed.' He'll repeat that over and over again." But, she says, "It's very difficult to think of putting someone in a residence when they're so nice. If they were rude and abusive," she says, it would be a different story. "But when they're so nice, and so loving, one feels terribly guilty to think about 'putting him off' as he puts it."

She says, "I am helped by having everybody at the cottage in the summer. When there's a lot of family and a lot of help, it doesn't seem necessary, but when I am alone with him again in the fall, I will have to do something else. It's physically and emotionally draining.

"When I imagine being alone with him, I feel that I can't provide everything that he needs. Right now, I'm sort of doing the work of imagining what a nursing home will be like and trying to adjust to that idea, that perceived loss, that perceived failure. It's hard not to feel those feelings. I feel that's my work now. I'm dealing with it. I'm anticipating it. I'm getting myself ready. I may not be there yet, but I anticipate it won't be too long."

My mother admits she is becoming worried about the toll taking care of my father has taken on her. "I already feel that I'm distracted. I can't remember everything I'm supposed to remember. I'm so stressed. I find it difficult to keep track of everything. I have to think of him first, all day long. When we go out to eat, I spend the first part of the meal figuring out what he's going to eat, and when the person comes to take the order, I haven't even thought about what *I'm* going to eat!"

If my father does not belong with us, where does he belong? I'm sure my mother has thought the same thing I have: he belongs at home, or nowhere at all. Many people who love my father wish that he would die before it's time for him to leave our home. That's why it's hard to even look at a brochure about a nursing home or memory care facility, much less walk in the door.

The options near my parents' home in Detroit and near our cottage in northern Michigan are traditional nursing homes, assisted living and special memory care facilities, and small foster care or residential homes. Though nothing geographically desirable seems like the perfect place for my father at this point, it is clear that the landscape of residential care options for people living with Alzheimer's is changing for the better across the United States. New options and revolutionary new kinds of care are becoming available as a result of the efforts of several visionaries. Someday, I hope these new attitudes toward caregiving and residential care will be evident everywhere.

One of the people helping to speed the revolution in Alzheimer's care is Joanne Koenig Coste, author of *Learning to Speak Alzheimer's: A Groundbreaking Approach for Everyone Dealing with the Disease.* She not only changed the way many people look at Alzheimer's when she described her own experiences of living with a husband with early-onset Alzheimer's, but she also continues to consult at nursing homes to help health care workers understand what people living with Alzheimer's are facing, how to give them better care, and how to make their facilities more humane. In her book, Koenig Coste describes the nightmare she lived with her husband, and how she changed the way she dealt with his disease.

Koenig Coste says Alzheimer's disease poses an unusual challenge when deciding whether someone might be better off being cared for by experts in a nursing home. "Promises made to others when the situation was simpler may be impossible to keep after Alzheimer's intrudes and causes tremendous changes. Disease complicates the decisions and necessitates new plans," Koenig Coste writes. "Use love as your guide. 'Do I love her enough, am I worried enough about her well-being, to have her be angry with me for a while if someone else can care for her better than I can?' For many patients and their families, home care is not the ideal option—everyone may be better able to thrive if the patient lives outside the family home."

In *Alzheimer's and Dementia: Questions You Have . . . Answers You Need*, Jennifer Hay devotes a chapter to how you know when it's time to move the person living with Alzheimer's out of the home. She writes that the decision to put someone in a residential facility "may be prompted by the physical and emotional health of the family caregivers. If the primary caregiver becomes physically ill or emotionally unable to continue caring for his loved one at home— if, for example, his stress level has reached a certain limit or other family members have reached limits of their own—the family may consider placing their loved one in a long-term care facility." Hay identifies one of the reasons the decision is so difficult, especially for spouses. "Nursing home placement marks an end to their previous life with their loved one. They know she will never again live with them at home." Hay says it is difficult for many caregivers to realize, but "relationships can continue and even improve once a family member has moved to a nursing home or other long-term care facility. The move can relieve family caregivers of the physical burdens and responsibilities of caregiving, allowing them to devote more time to meeting their loved one's emotional needs. Instead of spending two hours helping their loved one bathe and dress, they can spend two hours talking with her."

Moyra Jones, author of *Gentlecare: Changing the Experience of Alzheimer's Disease in a Positive Way*, is yet another revolutionary who has led the way in helping to change the way people who are living with Alzheimer's are treated. In her book, she describes Gentlecare this way: "a prosthetic system of dementia care designed to change the experience of a dementing illness such as Alzheimer's disease for those afflicted persons, their families, and professional caregivers." Her system is applicable to acute care institutions, long-term care facilities, and day care programs. She says, "It changes the way family caregivers see their role in a demented person's own home."

Jones writes, "In the Gentlecare system the person suffering from dementia is thought of as part of a family, and any intervention takes this into account. Gentlecare emphasizes that whole families, not just individuals, suffer from Alzheimer's disease. Effective dementia care must acknowledge the power of family by supporting and assisting family members, and involving them in the care process. If there is no existing family, it is sometimes necessary to create an artificial or surrogate family."

John Zeisel, president of Hearthstone Alzheimer Care and Hearthstone Alzheimer's Family Foundation, is trying to change how Alzheimer's patients are treated in nursing facilities. After completing his PhD in sociology at Columbia, he became a Loeb fellow at the Harvard Graduate School of Design. He is implementing his new ideas about taking care of people living with Alzheimer's and dementia at seven Hearthstone Homes in Massachusetts and New York. When I interviewed him in May 2007, he was writing a book called *I'm Still Here,* which he hoped would help to change the public perception of Alzheimer's disease.

The first thing Zeisel made clear to me was that he does not call a person with Alzheimer's an "Alzheimer's patient." He insisted that we use the phrase "a person living with Alzheimer's." His basic philosophy of caregiving is based on these tenets: meaning, compassion, and mindfulness. He incorporates a Buddhist philosophy into much of his work. He believes people living with Alzheimer's should not be placed in normal nursing home or assisted living routines. When it's time for them to go to a residential facility, he says, they should be part of programs like the one Hearthstone offers, designed specifically for people with the disease.

Zeisel is convinced that "people with Alzheimer's are creative, perceptive, and alive." He came up with an innovative approach to finding meaning and purpose in almost everything the person living with Alzheimer's comes into contact with throughout the day. The physical environment is specifically designed for people living with Alzheimer's—everything from open but safe gardens to give them total independence to hallways that have specific destinations with interesting objects on the walls to help them find their way. Bedrooms are filled with personal objects with special meaning to spark memories. They also have a view of, as well as access to, the out of doors so they can connect to the natural world and experience the weather and the sun and the moon. Common areas feel like home, says Zeisel, and include kitchens, living rooms, and dining rooms. "There are no extraneous sights and sounds or chaos. And then of course there is all the support a person living with Alzheimer's might need, like walking and getting to the toilet."

Zeisel says, "My big idea, my mission in life now, is to provide meaning in people's lives who are living with Alzheimer's. You can keep the vessel alive and open, but if there's nothing in it, you're just increasing the tragedy." According to Zeisel, after taking someone to a Hearthstone treatment residence, family members tell him that they "develop better relationships with the people they love who have Alzheimer's" than they had before.

I told Zeisel that my mother's biggest fear is that if we put my father into a nursing home, he would die. His answer surprised me. "If you put him someplace with no meaning, he *will* die. It's a different way of thinking about the world of Alzheimer's, even for people *with* Alzheimer's. We understand that people with the disease can still learn things and appreciate things." Zeisel believes that special qualities are actually unearthed in the person living with Alzheimer's as well as in their caregivers, what he calls "the gifts of Alzheimer's." For example, "all the good things you've seen your father be and do, that same attachment to life, continues in a different way, from the beginning to the end." Zeisel looks at the disease like this: "Although certain parts of the brain are damaged, the brain is very much there."

Hearthstone's approach is to "understand the person's history and memories. Many of the things he is are still in there. The program has to be organized to access what's in there already, to give residents challenges [so they can] continue to learn and improve. There are many ways to do this. One way is to form attachments. They still need the warmth of relationships. It's not as if you're handing him over to us. You're still taking care of him. We're just helping."

Zeisel is developing a Hearthstone Institute to consult with and train other facilities to develop the Hearthstone approach. He also started a program called Artists for Alzheimer's, which brings artists into places like Hearthstone residences and gets residents out to cultural centers such as the Museum of Modern Art and to see shows and other events such as the Big Apple Circus. Artists for Alzheimer's is spreading across the globe. Museums elsewhere in the United States and in France, Germany, and Australia are now involved, as well as some in the United Kingdom and Brazil. Unfortunately, there are only seven Hearthstone Alzheimer's treatment residences in the United States as of this writing, summer 2007. That is the kind of place I'd like my father to be, if only it were geographically feasible. You can find out more about Hearthstone and Artists for Alzheimer's at www.theHearth.org and www.ArtistsforAlzheimers.org.

Two other people working to improve the way people with Alzheimer's are treated are Dr. William Thomas and his wife, Jude Thomas. They started the Eden Alternative in 1992. I talked with Eden Alternative community builder, Carole Ende, who said the theory is "actually very simple: it's based on the theory that human beings were meant to live in a garden and not an institution. They need to live in a human habitat." In the 1990s, The Thomases pinpointed what they believed were the major problems in traditional nursing homes. They called them "the plagues of loneliness, helplessness, and boredom." According to Ende, the Thomases believe that those three plagues can actually kill people. The Eden Alternative is built on the idea that "relationships matter. Love matters. And so in human habitats, people take care of each other and help each other to grow."

There are now approximately 260 facilities in the United States and Canada on the Eden Alternative registry. Ende admits that it's hard work to become part of the program. The staff has to make a commitment to follow the tenets put forward by the Thomases of constantly building a community with meaning and close relationships. "We are not looking for thousands of homes to be on the registry. What we're looking for is the very best, a group of people working together to bring about this change." Ende describes the Eden Alternative philosophy as a commitment to cultural change and organizational transformation. Local schools are often involved with Eden homes on a regular basis. Staff members are encouraged to bring their pets in, and pets often live on the premises. According to Ende, an Eden home is like a "neighborhood, with a busy home life. There's a lot of effort involved." Like John Zeisel's Hearthstone theory, Eden requires "meaning everywhere, even in the pictures on the wall, wherever you look. There are stories attached to every item." A feeling of freedom in Eden homes is paramount. Everyone's favorite food is available, and everyone has refrigerator rights. In an Eden home, a person living with Alzheimer's is encouraged to be "in the moment, to be valued in society, to be the best human being you can possibly be." The Thomases are now bringing their theories about caring for people with Alzheimer's into the homes of caregivers and their loved ones, a program they call Eden at Home. You can find out more about the Eden Alternative at www.edenalt.com.

I decided to visit an Eden Alternative home named Grandvue not far from my parents' summer cottage. The building was perched on a hill with a view of a valley and forests below. I met with the certified activity director, Montessori instructor, and Eden associate, Mary Stahl. When we walked inside, several cats and dogs were in the hallway. There were brightly colored birds in cages. Activities seemed to be underway in every room. A choir rehearsed nearby. People in the hallways were talking together and doing projects.

Stahl walked into the interview accompanied by her dog, a Weimaraner named Lou. Stahl has been at Grandvue for three and a half years. She told me that approximately 30 percent of the residents at Grandvue have Alzheimer's. She believes the two main strengths of Grandvue are the Eden and Montessori methods.

"With the Montessori activity, we build on each individual person's strengths in the group. Everyone in the group has a social role, which makes everyone able to have a positive outcome." Stahl used the example of baking cookies, which they do every morning. "One person can still read recipes. Another measures well. Another is in charge of stirring. One person can turn on the oven. One might put the cookies on the tray to be baked. Even down to the critique, any way that they can have input in the group is what we build on.

"Montessori is the same principle as is used for children, but we modify it. We use items they would have used in their time. Montessori is hands-on learning versus memory learning, because with dementia they lose the ability to build on memory and they lose the ability to problem solve, so those are the things we don't want to focus on when we're doing activities. We want to focus more on the procedural memory, the things they learned early in life that just pop into their head. We find out what their strength is, whether it be gardening, cooking, or woodworking, or we create an activity that's broken down into individual steps."

The theory at Grandvue's dementia unit, Stahl says, is to "build independence." When they do activities together, "we use templates to show them. For example, if we were sorting silverware, we would have a template that would actually have the silverware pattern on it, we would show them how to do it, then ask them to do it. What we're trying to do is independently pattern that activity into their brain. Each time we can back off a little more and a little more, and then they're independently able to do the activity. It builds their self-esteem, and then they don't need constant redirecting."

What attracted me to Grandvue, and the combination of Montessori methods and the Eden Alternative philosophy, was the idea that people like my father can still learn and be involved in activities as long as possible. The people there are concerned about his pride and sense of self-worth, just as we are at home.

According to Stahl, at Grandvue "There's never any 'wrong.' If they've put the knives in with the forks, as long as they're actively engaged and having fun and it's meaningful, that's the key. That's what we do with Montessori. We're also an Eden facility, and that builds on relationships. Some of the tools we use for that are the plants and animals and children. We use those tools to build relationships."

The community surrounding Grandvue and, in particular, nearby schoolchildren are part of the experience. "We have two co-ops that come in, four- and five-year-olds, and one group works with the dementia unit. They do crafts together and they do lunch together." In addition to the ongoing relationships during the year with local schools, Grandvue has a volunteer program in the summer for local students, some of whom work up to forty hours a week. "We just started a program with job shadowing for high school students in the activities department," Stahl explained.

According to Stahl, music is extremely important at Grandvue. "We really try to build on music and we're so fortunate. On the dementia unit, two of my activity staff are excellent musicians. One plays the piano and sings. We have a large choir made up of the entire population here, and they perform at concerts. They have three major concerts a year. The dementia unit actually started the choir. There's vesper music, too. This month we're having a Johnny Cash party because there's someone here who plays that kind of music. We have a harmonica player."

I asked Stahl if she gets depressed doing the work she does. "I've never found it sad," she said. "It is very rewarding. I enjoy everything I do. As far as what I see is so important with our Alzheimer's or dementia patients, once we get them into a pattern or a structure, so they know that every day after breakfast we go to this one room and do an activity, once they got that pattern, we didn't have to go find them to bring them. They knew where to go. So to see them, that independence, instead of someone telling you what to do every minute, it was wonderful to see. They would get there and then the social part of the group started fitting in and the helping each other and building relationships, so the Eden and the Montessori [philosophies] kind of wove into each other. They started knowing when someone was missing. It kind of put them back into the world. It was really exciting."

Grandvue seems like a place in which my father might be happy until the end of his days—when my mother is ready, when my family is ready, when he is ready.

I visited another home in northern Michigan called Effie's Place with my parents. It is a beautiful gray house with white trim on a tree-lined avenue in a town called Leland. Blue morning glories wind up the pillars on the front porch. Even in late autumn, brilliant flowers and birdhouses fill the front yard. Music was wafting out of the living room windows as we approached the front door.

Moments after we arrived, a man wearing a beret and a red vest appeared from his room and headed to the piano in the living room. He sat down confidently and placed his age-spotted hands on the keys. He began playing jazz tunes such as "Autumn Leaves" and "My One and Only Love." We led my father to a chair next to the piano. My mother sat next to him. The man, whose name was Andy, began playing "Somewhere Over the Rainbow." My father smiled immediately, and he started to sing along. We learned only after our visit that Andy was in the later stages of dementia.

Effie's Place is a fairly new home, a place where a large family might reside. We realized even in those first few moments inside that in a way, this *is* a family. It's one of the only places like it in the state of Michigan and one of only a handful like it across the country. When we visited, about a third of the people there had Alzheimer's or some form of dementia. The house is in the middle of a small town along a lake within walking distance of the post office, library, museum, local restaurants, shopping, and coffee shops. It provides round-the-clock individualized care for eight people by a constant staff of two people on eight-hour shifts. They offer medication supervision; three meals a day; laundry services; weekly housekeeping; twenty-four-hour emergency response; several pets; and transportation to cultural, social, and recreational events.

My father seemed to enjoy the place and feel comfortable the minute he walked inside. I'm sure Andy's music at the piano made a difference. The fact that it didn't have an institutional feeling— nothing about it seemed like a nursing home—made a huge difference in how my mother and I felt about it, too. It seemed as though we were visiting someone's home for a party or a visit with friends. My father introduced himself to everyone in the house and started singing along with Andy right away. Because it felt like we were visiting someone's home, he didn't keep asking, "Why are we here?" or any of the questions he usually asks when we take him to day care facilities. The alarms in his brain that he's being "taken somewhere" or "put somewhere" didn't go off. He seemed the same way he was at home, sitting in his reclining chair.

Arden Schleuter, the owner and manager of Effie's Place, explained to us that they "wanted an assisted living residence with a homelike atmosphere. It's so difficult for people to leave their home. We wanted to ease that transition."

"Effie's place has a capacity of eight people," Schleuter said. "We wanted it to be that way. Residents have a mixture of everything from severe dementia to various physical issues." She explained that many people don't realize when they make the decision to move a loved one into residential care that at a home like Effie's Place, the residents "start taking the place of the family where the person with Alzheimer's used to live." This is one of the biggest benefits of a small residential facility like hers, she said, the bonding of staff and clients. "It becomes a family, and the residents start to take care of each other.

"We wanted to provide a setting with a homelike atmosphere where people can live their lives out with dignity, be loved and be cared for with dignity on a day-to-day basis. That's our goal." Schleuter says a place like Effie's makes families of Alzheimer's patients feel comfortable about the decision they've made. "You look around and think, okay, where would you want your parent to be? You would want them to be in a setting you knew and trusted. Not everybody has that luxury, whether they have Alzheimer's or heart failure or any other disease. It's very difficult to care for them at home.

"We give breakfast to people as they wake up," Schleuter said. No one is rousted from bed at an early hour. "They get up when they get up. We sometimes have people in the living room waiting for staff in the morning, and then some who don't get up until 10:30 in the morning. Lunch is at about 12:30. It's easygoing. Meals are not strict or set in stone. We meet different people's different needs. It's like having a large family." Sometimes the staff takes residents on a walk or for a drive. "In the early evening, everybody gathers in the living room. They have wine or cocktails if it's okay with the physician and the family. (Andy, the piano player, likes the local wine called Fishtown every night.) It's very social.

Dinner is usually at about 6:30. There's a big routine—to watch *Wheel of Fortune* and *Jeopardy!* or Lawrence Welk. There's bridge. Andy plays the piano. We have grilling outside, and we go on field trips. We go to the dunes, to the park, or we go for walks and go to the ice cream parlor."

Effie's Place is another kind of residence where I could imagine my father living. My mother even seemed to be able to visualize him being happy here. She said, "It's a family feeling. Because it's so small, people can help with the dinner preparations, people help set the table. Andy plays the piano. Woody was singing along. Because it's an actual house, it doesn't have an institutional feel. And I like the way Effie's takes advantage of the surrounding town." Unfortunately, it is more than an hour and a half drive from my parents' summer cottage. My mother says this is too far away because, if and when my father goes somewhere, she plans to visit him every day. However, if a place like Effie's were near my parents' year-round home or their summer cottage, I believe my mother would consider it.

In January 2007, I left my mother alone with my father for more than two weeks so I could write, do interviews and research, and have some time alone. As difficult as it was going to be, I was also allowing my mother to get a glimpse of what it would be like to take care of my father alone once I leave and go on with my life. It was the longest period of time I had been separated from my mother and father since I had come home more than two years ago. I talked frequently with my mother on the phone, and from her voice I could tell she was exhausted.

As I was getting ready to leave the cottage and go back home to help my mother, the phone rang. When I picked it up, for the first time, my mother said the words, "I'm ready."

Chapter Fourteen

Have Yourself a
Merry Little Christmas

THE HOLIDAYS SEEM TO BRING MY FATHER'S strengths and weaknesses to the forefront, and there are often wonderful surprises along the way. The last two Christmases I spent with my family were both a challenge and a treasure. Despite the fact that almost all of his memories are gone, my father continues to amaze me.

It's getting harder and harder to explain almost anything to him. Shopping, for instance, isn't a concept he seems to know anymore. But somehow the idea of Christmas, and the gift giving it requires, has remained in his head. We are now Christmas shopping. A light snow is coming down. I've explained what we're doing, where we're going, and whom we're buying for. Suddenly he asks, very upset, in a kind of panic, "Do I have something for my wife?" This is good news. Somewhere inside Dad's brain, it has registered that he needs to have a present for my mother. As we shop, I tell him, every ten minutes or so, that we have bought two beautiful things for her, presents wrapped with silver and red and green ribbon. I explain, again, that we are now buying a few more small items to put under the tree. The fact that we have bought the presents does not stay in his brain, but the knowledge that he needs to buy a present for Mom *is* in there.

We are in a long line to pay for our presents. He's uncomfortable standing in line, and he doesn't know what he should be doing or why we're there. Making small talk, trying to make him comfortable, I tell Dad for what is perhaps (this is not an exaggeration) the three hundredth time that it's Christmas and that we have a present for Mom.

Then I tell him, "Dad, something else special is coming up."

"What?" he asks.

"Your anniversary!" I say.

"Really?" he replies.

Then I ask a question he probably can't answer, which I usually don't do, and especially not in public, but I want to know what he remembers about being married to Mom. I ask, "How many years do you think you've been married?"

He says, "I don't know! Twenty-five?"

I tell him the news: "No, Dad, fifty-six!"

He looks shocked. I don't realize until then that, of course, the people behind us in line are hearing our conversation. What can they be thinking, listening to a man who can't remember anything about his own life?

Just then the woman standing right behind us, who has been privy to the entire conversation, puts her hand on my back and presses it between my shoulder blades, a gesture to tell me, "I know." I can feel her fingers pressing into me in a soft and gentle way. Then she leans into me, bends toward my ear, and in a sort of whisper says, "Bless you."

That's when I lose it for the first time in a long while. I haven't cried since I left New York, but at that moment, everything dissolves. I sob there in line. Dad looks at me, trying to figure out what is going on.

"Why are you crying?" he asks.

"Oh, just because it's the holidays," I say.

He says, "No, it's because of me."

Somehow I pay for the presents, and we get out to the snowy parking lot and back into my car. I still want to find out what Dad remembers about Mom even though it makes me sad. We're sitting in the car as the snow gets thicker and falls in big flakes onto the pavement. Finally I ask, "Why did you ask Mom to marry you?" He answers, without a pause or a beat, "Because she was perfect."

He didn't remember how many years he'd been married to her, he didn't remember that we'd already bought gifts for her, but he did remember why he loved her. Even when he has forgotten all our names, I have a feeling he will always remember my mother. She will be like a presence, a feeling he will always carry with him, part of his being, something that supports him, drives him, forms his very existence, like an invisible hand on his back, pushing him forward and helping to comfort him as he heads into the unknown.

Two Christmases ago, my father's singing group, the Grunyons, decided almost on a whim to attend an open audition to perform before the annual Radio City Music Hall Rockettes Christmas Show at the Fox Theatre in downtown Detroit. I don't think they believed they'd even make it to the final round, but their a cappella singing wowed the judges, and they were chosen to open the show. Even though my father had not participated in the competition, the Grunyons told my mother that he knew all the tunes they planned to sing, and they wanted him to be on stage with them.

My mother wasn't sure he should do it. It was a high-pressure situation. If Dad screwed up, it would make the Grunyons look bad in front of hundreds of people at a high-profile venue in downtown Detroit—at one of the most popular shows of the season. Would the benefit for my father, compared to the risk for the Grunyons, be worth it? Getting him ready to go would be difficult, and we wondered whether the Grunyons would be able to manage everything backstage. Already my mother and I were envisioning the ride to the theater and the repeated "Where are we going?" questions from Dad. Would he get nervous? Would he even understand what he was doing? Would he walk in the wrong direction and get lost in the huge theater? Would he trip getting up onto the stage? (Lately, his Alzheimer's is affecting his motor movements in more profound ways. He doesn't seem to lift his feet high enough these days, and he's tripping more often.) In the end, we decided he should, he *must* participate, because each day we realize this could be the last time.

Getting ready that day was difficult. My mother and I still don't know how to tie a tie—and Dad doesn't remember how to do it anymore. As predicted, he kept wondering what all the fuss was about. Then, when we got to the hall, there was confusion over the tickets. I parked the car while my parents went to the box office. Mom was still talking with the ticket agent when I got inside. I looked around and realized—no Dad!

Where was Dad? While Mom had been talking with the ticket agent, he had wandered off. My heart pounded. I looked outside. There he was, pacing back and forth in front of the theater, a look of panic in his eyes. I ran up to him and grabbed his hand.

"There you are!" he exclaimed. I pretended nothing was wrong—he is so sensitive to our moods that I have learned to exude calm even when I am upset about something. I pulled him inside the lobby. Mom got the tickets, and we proceeded to look for where his singing group might be gathering for the performance.

We finally found the rehearsal room, and his old friend and fellow baritone, Dick Bourez, tied the tie we had left dangling around Dad's collar. We left Dad in the Grunyons' steady hands, took two deep breaths, and went out into the hall to our seats. Then we got nervous. Very nervous.

As we waited for the Grunyons to appear on stage, I realized that Dad was probably going to pull this off just fine. I had a gut feeling that his years of experience as a performer would kick in and punch their way through his Alzheimer's.

The lights went down. The Grunyons filed out onto the huge, lighted stage. There was Dad, looking the way he always did when he sang with his group: confident, smiling. I watched him through-out the performance, and you can ask any of the Grunyons: Dad seemed to know his part and all the words. They sounded great, especially on "Have Yourself a Merry Little Christmas," one of Dad's favorites, which he often whistles and sings in any season. The audience cheered. The Grunyons gave a fantastic performance. They made sure my father got off stage without a problem. My mother was relieved. We both let out a big sigh.

Afterward, Dad got lost for the second time that evening trying to find his way to the bathroom. We found him after a few minutes of panic. We told him what a wonderful show it was—how great he sounded, how good he looked. Several Grunyons and members of the audience patted my father on the back and shook his hand.

"What did I do?" he asked.

I don't know if he remembered being on the stage, but I am quite sure, from the look on his face, that he knew something wonderful had happened. He seemed to stand up straighter than he had before. A smile seemed to come more easily to his lips. He said, "Aren't those great guys?" And then he asked, "Aren't we lucky?"

Mom and I said "Yes" in unison. I know we were both thinking, Yes, we are so lucky. We're so lucky to have you in our lives.

I am still not sure about the afterlife. I am convinced you are supposed to try to make this place down here as close to heaven as you possibly can, but there is one thing of which I am sure: if there is a heaven, my father will not get lost on his way there.

Chapter Fifteen

The Next Step

O<small>N</small> F<small>EBRUARY</small> 5, 2007, I <small>HAD BEEN</small> alone at our cottage on the lake for more than two weeks. This was the longest period of time I'd been away from Mom and Dad since I had come home from New York almost exactly two years ago. How strange. When I shopped for groceries by myself, without Dad driving the motorized cart and shouting "Following you!" and waving at the people in the aisles and smiling at the babies, and when I made the bed alone, I missed Dad. I also missed the relationship I had developed with my mother. I missed the talks we had together at night after Dad had gone to bed. I felt this weird kind of lonely I hadn't felt in so long. In fact, I suddenly realized I had not been alone for more than twenty-four hours for many months.

Much of my time away offered an incredible feeling of freedom. I could stay up all night if I wanted to. No schedule to keep. No taking Dad to adult day care at a certain time. No eating cereal with Mom and Dad at 9:30 a.m. No making sure he has Ensure with him before his lunch and that he takes his pills in the morning and at night. Life is so different without the routines that are necessary when you are living with someone with Alzheimer's.

I had to admit that I did not miss the trapped feeling that comes with helping to take care of someone who has Alzheimer's. It's like a strange depression that wraps around you and doesn't let go.

After this solitary time of writing and being alone and doing whatever I wanted to, whenever I wanted to, it was time to go back home to help my mother take care of my father. I scrubbed and cleaned and laundered everything possible at the cottage and delayed my departure for two entire days. I kept coming up with excuses to keep from going home, back to the schedule, back to the sadness, back to being a daughter again. Finally, I couldn't put it off any longer. It was time to go. I scrubbed the kitchen sink twice. I vacuumed the rug twice, too. I packed my car. I turned down the thermostats. I took out the last bag of garbage. I set the alarm. I turned the key in the door. I walked out to the car. Then I went back in. I kept going out the door of our cottage and coming back in. I'm sure I was trying to think of a reason not to go. I checked the thermostats again, made sure the draft was closed on the fireplace. A snowstorm was bearing down on northern Michigan. The roads were bad. There were whiteouts. Couldn't I stay just one more day? I could have. The weather and road conditions were excuse enough.

I had already bought more time, a few more days of this luxurious feeling of being alone. I knew from the sound in my mother's voice that she was exhausted from taking care of Dad alone for so long and needed relief. This time, though, I thought, Why is this my problem? It's her choice to keep him home! It was the first time I had felt this way. It was like an alarm had gone off—an alarm that said, I can't do this anymore.

I didn't used to feel this way.

For the past two years I had felt responsible. I had *wanted* to be responsible. I even enjoyed the role I had taken on. It was something I had signed up for. Now, suddenly, something in me had let go. I wonder sometimes if I came home because of unfinished business with my mother and father; if maybe it was I who needed them more than they needed me. Now that I had fulfilled some sort of unspoken obligation, I could go on with my life on my own in a more complete way. As I closed the door of the cottage for the last time, I realized that perhaps something about stepping into my parents' lives to help out in this time of crisis had set me free in a way I had never been free before.

Finally, I drove away, past the hemlocks and pines and birches and the snow-filled lane. Big, soft flakes that looked like giant confetti came down on my car as I drove away. I was glad I had lost my cell phone in a snowdrift. For about an hour, I enjoyed a quiet I hadn't experienced in so long. Then I turned on the radio and listened to the news and just drove and breathed in being alone some more. I knew I wouldn't feel this alone again for quite some time.

I pulled up to my parents' house. I took a deep breath, and then I just stayed in my jeep in the driveway for a few moments before I walked in the door. When I walked inside, Mom's hair was fixed beautifully. She wore makeup and lipstick and a matching sweater and pants. She looked fantastic. I don't know how she does it. I believe my face becomes stressed and strained and gains a few more wrinkles from being with Dad alone for just a few hours. I had left her alone with Dad for more than two weeks, and she seemed radiant. The house was immaculate. She had made dinner for us to eat during half time of the Super Bowl. This time, Mom was sitting in Dad's reclining chair because he forgot he sits there. He was sitting on the couch, which is usually my mother's place. I was afraid to see Dad when I walked in the door because I was afraid he might not know me this time. I was afraid of what I might not see in his eyes. And I was afraid of the feeling I was going to have of wanting to go back out the door, of wanting to get away, rather than go back to that trapped feeling again.

When I talked with my father on the phone the last time before I left the cottage, I reported to him what I had been doing and told him I would be coming home. He said, "I'm so glad you're coming home so I can love you again!" Is this why I came home, so he can love me again? And yet having my father love me again has come with a price. This time, when I walked in the door, I felt like it was a very large price—having my own life.

When Dad got up from the couch where he was watching the television, I saw that he knew me and most likely placed me in a spot in his heart and mind where family and people he loves go. But he still didn't know my name. He looked so bent over with that lion look. It's difficult to explain what I call Alzheimer's Effect. Something in his face looked slack. Because his eyes don't sparkle as much or focus in the same way, it's not like connecting with another human being the way it used to be, because, as he would say, he is "broken inside."

He is eighty now, I kept saying to myself as I watched him come toward me, but it was more than his aging that struck me. In the past two weeks of not seeing him, not singing with him, not doing our word exercises or our physical exercises, he seemed to become someone else. It was as if the muscle that was the two of us over the past two years hadn't been exercised and had begun to atrophy. Our connection seemed to be ripping apart without the constant nurturing I had dedicated to it. I realized he didn't really remember that I had gone away.

He helped me carry a few things from the car. Because it was zero degrees, he kept repeating "It's cold!" When he came inside, he sat in his reclining chair this time (maybe the three of us remind him of the way we've been sitting together in front of the TV for two years, so now he remembered his place). As we sank into our spots in the chair and on the couch, I had a sinking feeling, too. Back to the repetition and monotony of helping take care of someone who has Alzheimer's. Back to our same places in the house, back to our same chairs, back to our same lives.

I didn't want to be back. I wanted to be alone again with my own patterns, to be able to stay up all night long if I wanted to, to write or read all night, take a bath at midnight, not have to wake up at any particular time, or even turn on the TV at 3 a.m without worrying about waking anyone up. That was the way I had lived in L.A., San Francisco, and New York.

I signed up for this. I chose it. I wanted to try to help my father and mother for as long as I could. But two years into it, I felt I couldn't do it anymore. Yet I couldn't see my way out of it, for me, or for my mother. I couldn't see the next step.

Chapter Sixteen

The Pear Trees

SOMETIMES I THINK I CAME HOME TO pretend the world wasn't coming to an end. But it is—the world with my father in it anyway. It has been two and a half years since I began helping my mother take care of my father. We are up north at the cottage. On this still, calm night, my father's whistling resounds throughout the house and out to the glassy lake.

"Where did I come from?" That's what my father has been saying for the past two days. "What do you mean, Dad?" we say. "Do I live here?" he says. "In the summer," one of us says. We explain that our family is here, together, for the next two months, and that in the fall he will go back to our house near Detroit. We tell him that he and Mom have been doing this for fifty-six years. Nothing registers in his eyes. "Did I ever have a job?" he says. This is weird because last week when someone asked him what he used to do for a living, he said, "I was president of E and E Engineering" clear and strong.

Tonight there is a full moon creeping up behind the trees. I walk to the end of the dock to look at the stars. The sky is clear and endless and sparkling, and I think about how when I look at these stars against the dark blackboard of sky, I know where they burn out of, I know that the closest star outside our solar system is 4.3 light-years away, and I know that through a jumble of DNA and a cacophony of events, somehow, we are down here on this earth. Though it has taken me some time, with the help of my father and mother over the past two and a half years, I may have finally figured out where I belong.

But where, through the tangle of Alzheimer's, are the identity markers, the distances of space, for my father? When he looks up at the night sky, does he even feel wonder at the moon and the stars, or are they just a sparkling ceiling, some fancy wallpaper to him? When he says, "Where did I come from? How did I get here?" is he trying to say to us, "I don't know where I live"? Or is he saying, "I don't know where I originated from"? Is it possible he is asking the larger question of his very existence?

I wonder often about how lost he must feel. Yet, his Alzheimer's has allowed him to ask deep questions about his existence at the same time that he is becoming lost to himself in the universe. Sometimes I think Alzheimer's has opened this portal to his brain that lets him ask the existential questions he has always wanted to ask. Maybe when he says, "Where did I come from?" he is really saying, "I don't know where I belong." Do any of us know, really? Maybe Alzheimer's just makes the feeling of being lost stronger, more pronounced. "Where did I come from?" my father says again, and I think, Where did any of us come from, really?

It is 9:30 p.m. "Where do I go now?" Dad asks. I say, "To your bedroom down the hall." He is lost now, almost all the time.

In what I believe will be the last summer I will help take care of my father, I walk at dusk through the woods near our cottage on the lake. A sudden wind howls through the trees. I see the poplar leaves shimmy. I watch the birch trees flail their limbs. An indigo bunting appears and sits regally in the top of a tree, then trills its cry, "sweet, sweet, cheer, cheer, fire, fire," nearby. I think about how the names of all the trees and flowers and birds have always meant so much to my family, and how my father doesn't know the names of any of these things anymore.

I wonder, Can he still feel great love? Can he feel emotional pain? I wonder if he will ever know the ache of his own heart again. Perhaps his heart aches all the time, and he can't tell us because he's "broken inside." I know he will never have the sense again of his own power. As he lets go of his memories, we let go of him. I am finally ready to say good-bye.

We have been looking at nursing homes. We have been talking about how to tell when it's time. We have been talking about the emotional and physical toll that having my father at home is taking on my mother. But he is so sweet, whistling as he sits on the couch, helping to fold laundry, telling my mother he loves her, asking her if he could help in any way, telling us he loves us. How could we take him somewhere? How could he be anywhere but with us?

The family is paralyzed. My mother, most of all, seems as if she is caught in amber, petrified, unable to move, wanting to have her world encased and frozen in time so she doesn't have to move from this space, or take the next heartbreaking step. There are times I think we keep him here with us for *us*, not for him. I am not sure anymore that this is the place he should be. I am not sure anymore that we can give him what he needs.

Sometimes I wish my father could say my name, instead of saying "Daughter," but I know he doesn't know my name anymore. He lists everyone in our family (a routine he and I go through every day), the names of his daughters, sons-in-law, and grandchildren. It is an amazing feat. From what I have read, it is something that he probably shouldn't be able to do anymore. He always says the names perfectly: Libby, Alison, Gary, Charlie, Nathan, Will, Bill, Rosemary, Mary Ellen. Sometimes he even remembers Rosie the dog. I am glad he knows all the names, but at the same time, there is something depressing about the list he reads off so well. We are simply part of a list of names to him. He can't decipher the differences between us anymore. When he says Mary Ellen, he doesn't know it's me, even when I am sitting next to him.

I just want a few lucid moments with him, just one more time. It isn't rational. It makes no sense, I know. It seems selfish. I know it isn't important in the scheme of things, but I just want him to say my name when he looks at me one last time instead of saying "Daughter." I would like to be able to tell him what an honor it has been to be with him these last two and a half years, and to know he understands how much he means to me and what a wonderful father he has been.

The pear trees in the front yard of the house where we grew up on a country road are more than one hundred years old. They are peeling and cracking, and the bark is falling off in chunks. The smooth, pale trunks show through the decaying bark. They are gnarled and beautiful. They still bloom and bear fruit, but when you look at them, you can't understand how they could create anything at all. Most of the trunks and branches are dead. On each tree, there are only a few spots that contain the cambium layer to carry nutrients and moisture to the top.

In every season since I've come home, my mother says, "We should just cut them down! They hardly bear fruit anymore! They're old and craggy looking and ugly, and the branches break off even in a small wind." But she never takes the step to rip them up out of the ground. I love them. The few blossoms are so singularly beautiful in spring—pungent, sweet, and soft. They broadcast the coming of plump pears, however imperfect they may be.

These craggy trees cast crooked shadows on the snow on gray winter days. When we were little, they guided all three of us daughters to the bus stop on chilly mornings. They stand like scarecrows guarding our yard, in autumn. Ghosts and goblins seem to run among them at Halloween. When snow falls, they stand like dark soldiers in formation on a white blanket, guiding people to our wreath-decorated door. In autumn, the few pears they do bear are abnormal, and the ants seem to get to them before we do. Even though there are only a handful of pieces of fruit, and they are often deformed, my mother collects them, peels and slices them, and makes pear butter with them anyway.

On this particular spring day, the pear trees are sending out new blossoms on one or two misshapen branches. They look like old ladies wearing fancy lingerie. It is an odd sight—dead branches and a flurry of white blossoms. On this day, we had finally done it: My mother, my father, and I had walked into a nursing home, and my mother had filled out the forms and met with administrators and nurses and given them medical information so my father can go there when it's time.

My mother drove home alone in her car. My father was in my jeep with me. It seemed as though the sky agreed with our assessment of this next possible step in our lives. Dark, threatening clouds moved in. There were high wind warnings, and the sky turned a mixture of black and yellow, like a giant bruise across the horizon behind the black silhouettes of trees. You could feel the pressure in the air, and then the sudden release with the gusts of wind.

As my father and I turned onto our road, the wind clawed at the old pear trees, tearing branches from the trunks. Large and small branches of the pear trees flew in front of us, almost landing on our car. The pieces were strewn across the driveway.

I asked Dad to get out of the jeep and move them off. (I will never know why I didn't get out of the car to do it myself.) He couldn't remember how to open the car door. I reached across his lap impatiently and pulled the door handle. When he got outside, even though branches were all around him on the ground, he couldn't understand what I wanted him to do. "Go there?" he said, and pointed to the mailbox. "No, Dad!" I shouted above the wind. "Move the branches so I can get by!" He finally bent down and picked up a branch. "This?" he shouted as the wind whipped around him and the sky got darker. He stood there holding the branch in his hands, looking confused.

I shouted out my window too loudly, "Take the branches and just throw them aside. Put them on the lawn so I can drive by." But he couldn't understand. Then a strange thing happened: He moved in front of my jeep. He centered his body a few inches from the bumper and he wouldn't move. There he was, standing in the middle of the driveway, holding the dead branches in his hands, refusing to get out of the way. I got very frustrated and shouted, "Dad, move! I have to get the car in the driveway!" At first, he looked confused, holding the broken branches in his hands with the yellow-gray sky behind him. Then he looked defiant. I wondered for a moment if he was trying to say, "I'm not going!" Or, "I'm not ready!" Maybe he was saying, "Recognize me as I go!"

I will never know why that happened, or what he was trying to say. If only he could have jumped through the plaque in his brain, Superman-like, leaping through the beta amyloid, igniting the neurotransmitters for just a moment, to explain.

The headlights of the car reflected in his watery-blue eyes. For a moment, his eyes looked wild. I got scared. This is it! I thought. He's going to throw himself in front of the jeep, holding those pear branches in his hands!

He refused to step aside. We were having a father–daughter standoff in the branch-strewn driveway in the middle of a storm. Then I thought, Maybe he wants me to run him over. I put the jeep in gear and I swerved around him. He looked bewildered, standing in our driveway, holding the broken branches in his hands, the yellow-gray sky behind him, his eyes reflecting in the headlights. Then he put the branches down and came inside.

That night, as I was helping him get ready for bed, giving him his pills, putting out his toothbrush with toothpaste on it, he stopped suddenly and pressed his head against mine in a different, cuddly way, not his usual way of showing affection. As he pressed his head against mine, he said, "I think I'm going to be without you soon." I choked up. I held his head against mine. I stayed quiet, holding his head, for some time.

I asked him what he meant. He said, "I don't know. I'm peculiar." I asked him to explain about being peculiar. "I'm getting worse," he said. Then I asked him to explain what he meant about being without me. He said, "What do you mean?" I repeated what he said. "Did I say that?" he exclaimed. The thought seemed to be gone. Dissipated. Like smoke from a candle. Like stars burning out from the sky. Like a song being sung for the last time.

Resources

Organizations

The Alzheimer's Association
info@alz.org
1-800-272-3900
225 North Michigan Avenue, 17ᵗʰ floor
Chicago, IL 60601-7633

National Alliance for Caregiving
www.caregiving.org
1-800-896-3650
4720 Montgomery Lane, 5ᵗʰ floor
Bethesda, MD 20814

Family Caregiver Alliance
www.caregiver.org
1-800-445-8106
180 Montgomery Street, Suite 1100
San Francisco, CA 94104

National Council on Aging
www.ncoa.org
202-479-1200

1901 L Street, NW, 4th floor
Washington, D.C. 20036

National Association of Area Agencies on Aging
www.n4a.org
202-872-0888
1730 Rhode Island Avenue, NW, Suite 1200
Washington, D.C. 20036

Eldercare Locator
www.eldercare.gov
1-800-677-1116

Aging Parents and Elder Care
Senior Solutions of America, Inc.
www.aging-parents-and-elder-care.com
P.O.Box 22123
Sarasota, FL 34276

Hearthstone Alzheimer Care
www.thehearth.org
1-888-422-CARE
23 Warren Avenue, Suite 140
Woburn, MA 01801

The Eden Alternative
www.edenalt.org
512-847-6061
111 Blue Oak Lane
Wimberley, TX 78676

Ami Simms and the Alzheimer's Art Quilt Initiative
www.AlzQuilts.org
4206 Sheraton Drive
Flint, MI 48532

American Association of Retired Persons (AARP)
www.aarp.org

National Academy of Elderlaw Attorneys: www.naela.org

Books and Publications

Caring Today magazine
www.caringtoday.com
203-254-0783
34 Sherman Court
Fairfield, CT 06824

Alzheimer's Daily News: www.alznews.org

The 36-Hour Day: A Family Guide to Caring for Persons with Alzheimer's Disease by Nancy L. Mace and Peter V. Rabins

Learning to Speak Alzheimer's: A Groundbreaking Approach for Everyone Dealing with the Disease by Joanne Koenig Coste

Alzheimer's: A Caregiver's Guide and Sourcebook by Howard Gruetzner

Moving a Relative with Memory Loss: A Family Caregiver's Guide by Laurie White and Beth Spencer

Gentlecare: Changing the Experience of Alzheimer's in a Positive Way by Moyra Jones

Alzheimer's and Dementia: Questions You Have . . . Answers You Need by Jennifer Hay

Other

Stephen M. Aronson, MD
734-973-9700
2020 Hogback Road
Ann Arbor, MI 48105

The Grunyons
web.mac.com/anthony.alcantara/iWeb/Grunyons/

The Alzheimers Store: Unique products and information for
    caregivers
www.alzstore.com
1-800-752-3238

Bibliography

Fackelmann, Kathleen. "Caregiving Keeps Alzheimer's Patients Home." *USA Today*, November 13, 2006.

Family Caregiver Alliance. "Caregiver Depression: A Silent Health Crisis." 2002. http://www.caregiver.org/caregiver/jsp/content_node.jsp?nodeid=786

Gross, Jane. "Forget the Career. My Parents Need Me at Home." *New York Times*, November 24, 2005.

Gruetzner, Howard. *Alzheimer's: A Caregiver's Guide and Sourcebook*. New York: John Wiley and Sons, Inc., 2001.

Harvard Health Publications. "A Guide to Alzheimer's Disease." http://www.health.harvard.edu/special_health_reports/A_Guide_to_Alzheimers_Disease.htm

Hay, Jennifer. *Alzheimer's and Dementia: Questions You Have . . . Answers You Need*. People's Medical Society, 1996.

Jones, Moyra. *Gentlecare: Changing the Experience of Alzheimer's Disease in a Positive Way*. Harley and Marks Publishers, Inc., 1999.

Kerwin, Diana. "With Alzheimer's, The Caregiver Is a Patient, Too." Medical College of Wisconsin Healthlink. http://healthlink.mcw.edu/article/1031002313.html

Koenig Coste, Joanne. *Learning to Speak Alzheimer's: A Groundbreaking Approach for Everyone Dealing with the Disease*. Boston: Houghton Miflin, 2003.

Levine, Carol, Ed. *Always On Call: When Illness Turns Families Into Caregivers*. Nashville: Vanderbilt University Press, 2004.

Lokvig, Jytte, and John D. Becker, MD. *Alzheimer's A to Z: A Quick Reference Guide*. Oakland, CA: New Harbinger Publications, Inc., 2004.

Mace, Nancy L., and Peter V. Rabins. *The 36-Hour Day: A Family Guide to Caring for Persons with Alzheimer's Disease.* Baltimore: John Hopkins University Press, 2006.

Sacks, Oliver. *Musicophilia: Tales of Music and the Brain.* New York: Knopf, 2007.

University of Michigan Museum of Zoology Animal Diversity Web site. "Birds." www.animaldiversity.ummz.umich.edu

White, Laurie, and Beth Spencer. *Moving a Relative with Memory Loss: A Family Caregiver's Guide,* second edition. Santa Rosa, CA: Whisp Publications, 2006.

Acknowledgments

I would like to thank my mother, Rosemary, for her insight, her patience, and all the memories she was so generous in sharing with me because my father could not. I would also like to thank my sisters, Alison and Libby, for letting me write this, and for their support and love throughout the process of helping my mother take care of my father as well as writing this book. My sisters; my brothers-in-law, Gary and Bill; and my nephews, Charlie, Will, and Nathan, took over care of my father on many occasions so that I could have time to write and so that my mother could have free time as well. Thank you for the respite.

There are so many people who helped me and believed in me along the way. My agent, Bonnie Nadell, helped to put me on this path and to navigate my way. My editor, Karen Murgolo, was perceptive, patient, and thoughtful throughout. I would also like to thank Jane Gross at the *New York Times*, whose beautiful article about my family touched so many hearts and sparked the germ of this book. My gratitude also goes out to Crys Quimby, the program director at WCBS Radio, without whom this book would never have happened; as well as WCBS vice president and general manager, Steve Swenson; and WCBS news director, Tim Scheld. Susan Strecker Richard at *Caring Today* magazine helped me in so many ways as well as Dian Wilkins at the Greater Michigan chapter of the Alzheimer's Association. I am indebted to Dr. Oliver Sacks and Kate Edgar for shining a light on my father and other Alzheimer's patients for whom music provides a lifeline, and I shall be forever grateful to Dr. Sacks for the foreword to this book. I would also like to thank Keith Taylor, Thomas Lynch, and Bret Lot at the Bear River Writer's Workshop; my father's singing group, the Grunyons; and the Pageturners and the rest of the congregation at the Paint Creek Unitarian Church.

There are many others who helped along the way, including John Stewart, Margaret Manos, Sara Smith and the Heartbreak Hotel, Mardi Link, Susan Denzer, Ceci Bauer, Michaelynn Meyers, Suzy Drell, Paige Simpson, the Frehses—Bob, Dale, Rob, Jessica, Woody, and Susan—Moses Londinski, and Dave and Linda Beier. And special thanks to Buzz Jenks for his support and patience throughout this process, and for always coming back, despite everything.

Finally, I want to thank my father. I believe he reached through his Alzheimer's to help me tell this story.

About the Author

MARY ELLEN GEIST was most recently the afternoon anchor at WCBS Radio in New York, which is the flagship station of CBS Radio and CBS News. Prior to that she was the morning anchor and reporter at KGO Radio in San Francisco and a reporter in Los Angeles. She lives on a lake in Northern Michigan.